WRIGHTSLAW

Special Education Legal Developments and Cases 2019

Peter W.D. Wright, Esq.
Pamela Darr Wright, MA, MSW

Wrightslaw

Special Education Legal Developments and Cases 2019

Peter W. D. Wright, Esq.

Pamela Darr Wright, MA, MSW

Harbor House Law Press, Inc.
Hartfield, Virginia 23071

Wrightslaw: Special Education Legal Developments and Cases 2019
By Peter W. D. Wright and Pamela Darr Wright
Library of Congress Cataloging-in-Publication Data
Wright, Peter W. D. and Pamela Darr Wright
Wrightslaw: Special Education Legal Developments and Cases 2019
p. cm.

ISBN 13: 978-1-892320-49-0
ISBN 10: 1-892320-49-5

1. Law — Special Education — United States.
2. Children with disabilities — Education — United States.
3. Special education — Parent Participation — United States. I. Title.

10 9 8 7 6 5 4 3 2 1

Printing History

Harbor House Law Press, Inc. issues new editions to keep our publications current. New editions include major revisions of text and/or changes. New printings include minor changes and corrections.

First Edition July 2020

Disclaimer

The purpose of this book is to educate and inform. Although efforts have been made to ensure that the publication is accurate, there may be mistakes, typographical and in content. If you are dissatisfied with this book, please return it to the publisher for a full refund.

When You Use a Self-Help Law Book

Law is always changing. The information contained in this book may or may not reflect current legal developments. For legal advice, you should consult with an attorney.

Bulk Purchases

Books published by Harbor House Law Press. Inc. are available at a discount for bulk purchases, academic sales and textbook adoptions. For information, contact Harbor House Law Press at (877) 529-4332 or at P. O. Box 480, Hartfield, VA 23071. Please provide the title of the book, ISBN number, quantity, how the book will be used, and date needed.

Toll Free Phone Orders:	(877) LAW IDEA or (877) 529-4332
Toll Free Fax Orders:	(800) 863-5348
Email:	orders@harborhouselaw.com
Website Orders / Online Store:	https://www.wrightslaw.com/store/index.html
Student discounts:	https://www.wrightslaw.com/bks/stu.discount.htm

Individual Purchases

The print edition of this book is available from Amazon. The PDF edition of this book is only available from Harbor House / Wrightslaw.com at: https://www.wrightslaw.com/store/2019law.html.

Dedication

This book is dedicated to the **Council of Parent Attorneys and Advocates** (https://www.copaa.org/). In 1998 Pam and I were part of the original group that formed COPAA. It's mission then and now "is to protect and enforce the legal and civil rights of students with disabilities and their families. The primary goal is to secure high quality educational services and to promote excellence in advocacy."

In our newsletter to help promote its first conference, we wrote that "COPAA is not a conference for theorists to discuss what should be, but is for the warriors who will fight battles in the trenches and the generals who will map strategy knowing what it is and how to do it. Applied techniques, tactics, strategy, war stories - it's all there at COPAA!" In 2020 it continues its dominant presence.

Acknowledgements

The COPAA members below edited this publication and provided valuable ideas and assistance.

Sabrina Axt, the mother of a child with dyslexia, has been practicing law in California since 2005. Having gone through the special education process with her own child, she developed a passion for helping other parents and students navigate the special education process. She now exclusively practices special education law and advocacy, working with parents to develop a strategy and plan to get their children the individualized support they need.
Hyperlink: https://www.axtlegal.com/

Missy Alexander is a Parent Educator, a Data Manager with The Parents' Place of Maryland, Maryland's PTI & F2F HIC and parent of a daughter on the autism spectrum. She is a former Chair of COPAA and is on their Board of Directors. We have had a close friendship with Missy since the late 1990's.
Parents Place hyperlink: https://www.ppmd.org/

Roy T. Atwood, the father of a child with Down syndrome, has been practicing law in Texas since 1988. He is a frequent speaker on litigation-related topics, teaches in trial skills programs and is the past president of the board of trustees of LaunchAbility, which helped people with developmental disabilities lead fulfilling lives. Last year it merged with "My Possibilities" and Roy is on their Board of Directors. He is passionate about providing opportunities for people with special needs. He has assisted many parents from creation of the Individualized Education Program, to placement in the least restrictive environment, due process hearings, and court appeals.
Hyperlink: http://atwoodgameros.com/

Danielle Green began practicing law in Massachusetts in 2007. As a result of her own experience with her

son and the school district, she developed a passion for special education advocacy, believing that a "collaborative approach between teachers, administrators, and parents is the best place to start in this process, but in certain circumstances having legal support is necessary."
Hyperlink: https://forexceptionalchildren.com

Calvin Luker has been a lawyer since 1981 and concentrates exclusively on issues related to people with disabilities. For ten years he worked with the Michigan's Protection and Advocacy Service. His practice is limited to special education; end of life issues; fair housing law; guardianship/ conservatorship law; juvenile justice; and other legal areas when they directly impact his clients with disabilities.

Patricia Luker developed her expertise in special education, community supports and parent advocacy in 1975. She has been the Director of Training at Michigan Protection and Advocacy Service, the Director of Family Services for Michigan's Parent Training and Information Center, and created and managed parent training programs for the Epilepsy Foundation of Michigan. She is the Senior Staff Advocate, The Arc of Oakland County.

Calvin Luker and Patricia Luker created the The Respect ABILITY Law Center in 2001 to advance the civil, service and support rights of and for people with disabilities and their families. The Respect ABILITY Law Center is a founding member of the Alliance to Prevent Aversive Intervention and Seclusion [APRAISE], a national organization dedicated to the enactment and implementation of national legislation to eliminate the use of seclusion, restraint and aversives in all schools.
Hyperlinks: http://www.respectabilitylawcenter.com/ and https://www.thearcoakland.org/

Table of Contents

How to Purchase and use this hyperlinked E-book PDF

Wrightslaw: Year in Review 2019 is available for purchase (immediate download) as a searchable e-book (PDF) from Wrightslaw at https://www.wrightslaw.com/store/2019law.html

When you see a case in the Table of Cases, you can click on the link that will take you to a summary of the case in Chapter 5.

All hyperlinks in the PDF download are active and show up on screen only when your cursor hovers over the link and becomes the image of a hand.

This page intentionally left blank.

Introduction

In 1997, when we began our website, Wrightslaw.com, information about legal issues related to special education was hard to find. Subscriptions to legal journals were expensive.

In 1998, when we published our first book, ***Wrightslaw: Special Education Law***, we hoped it would encourage more people to begin advocating for children with disabilities and that ordinary people would realize that special education law and advocacy isn't as complicated as it might appear. The success of that book was remarkable.

In 2006, as we wrote the introduction for the second edition of ***Wrightslaw: Special Education Law, 2nd Ed.***, we marveled at the increasing demand for training in special education law and advocacy.

We have been touched by how many people still rely on our website and our books, now, more than 20 years after creation of our website and publication our first book, ***Wrightslaw: Special Education Law***.

More parents, related service providers, educators, lay advocates and lawyers have turned to advocacy as it became clear that many schools were failing to provide children with disabilities with a free appropriate education.

This shift may also be due to a greater awareness of the high price that families, children and society pay when schools fail to provide "a free appropriate public education" (FAPE) that emphasizes "special education and related services designed to meet their unique needs and **prepare them for further education, employment, and independent living.**"[1]

Many attorneys and advocates initially entered this field as they advocated for their own child with special needs and experienced unexpected obstacles and challenges. Later, many then used their knowledge and experience to help other families.

In light of the increased interest in special education law and legal issues, we decided it was time to create a series of annual "year-in-review" books that focus on emerging caselaw from the Courts of Appeal. ***Wrightslaw: Special Education Legal Developments and Cases 2019*** is the fifth book in this series. In addition to the U.S. Supreme Court (SCOTUS), the landmark case law that changes the future is created in the U.S. Courts of Appeal.

Since 1997 and creation of our website, it has become much easier to find reliable information and cases. Google Scholar is a terrific tool, making legal research easier and free to all.

We hope these books will inspire a new generation of attorneys and advocates and be useful to seasoned veterans.

Why You Need This Book

If you are the parent of a child with a disability, you represent your child's interests. To be an effective ad-

1 This is the purpose of the special education statute. See 20 USC § 1400(d). It is the mission statement of the Individuals with Disabilities Education Act (IDEA).

vocate, you need to know about recent legal developments and cases that may affect your child's right to a special education program that is appropriate for your child.

If you work as a teacher, related service provider, or school administrator, you need to be aware of new developments in special education law.

If you are an attorney or advocate for children with disabilities and their families, you have a responsibility to stay current on special education case law and other legal issues that affect children with disabilities and their families.

How this Book is Organized

Chapter One includes an overview of legal terms, concepts, and federal statutes related to children with disabilities and special education law. You will learn about the four types of law and about federal laws that govern the education of children with disabilities.

Chapter Two describes the legal process —the steps in resolving a special education dispute — from the initial request for a due process hearing through appeals to federal courts and the U.S. Supreme Court (SCOTUS).

In Chapter Three, you will learn to use Google Scholar as a tool to find cases relevant to your interests and needs.

Chapter Four is the Table of Cases from the Courts of Appeal in 2019. The Table of Cases lists all significant cases in 2019, with the date, court, issues, outcome, and a short summary. Each case is hyperlinked to a discussion of the case in Chapter 5.

Chapter Five includes discussions of all significant cases from the Courts of Appeal in 2019. In these discussions, we use text that is "copied and pasted" from the decisions. Chapter Five also includes a report from the Government Accounting Office to Congress and three U.S. District Court cases.

Strategies to Help You Develop Expertise in Special Education Law

To develop expertise in special education law, you need to read cases from the U.S. District Courts and U.S. Courts of Appeal. As you do this, you will want to look up the statute or regulation at issue and, if you have our law book, cross-reference the case. This is a long slow road, but you can't avoid it. You must read cases to understand legal issues, outcomes, and why a case is significant.

As you begin to educate yourself, you may be tempted to read articles about a case, instead of reading the actual case. When you read an article, you are reading the authors' words. An author's words often reflect that person's personal biases.

If you read **about** a case, you limit your understanding of the case. You need to read the Judges' words to understand the Court's reasoning for their decision. In ***Wrightslaw: Special Education Legal Developments and Cases 2019,*** we rely on direct quotes from the decisions – the Judges' words.

If you want to learn more about a case that is in this book, use Google Scholar to find the earlier District Court opinion that was appealed. Read that earlier decision and then, again, read the decision by the Court of Appeals.

To understand the law, you must take the hard road. Read original opinions several times. Do not rely on the opinions and summaries of others. If you take these steps, you will develop expertise in special education law.

> *Learning from the past helps our understanding the evolutions of things and can also give insights into the future.* (Link to source is here.)

To further develop your expertise in special education law and legal issues, we recommend that you begin with the first book in this series, ***Wrightslaw: Special Education Legal Developments and Cases 2015.***

As you read the ***Wrightslaw: Special Education Legal Developments and Cases*** books, you don't have to do a detailed analysis of each case. Skim and read the cases for enjoyment. You will quickly see that judicial writing styles vary. Some cases read like a novel, opening with a "hook" to get your interest and motivate you to read the case through to the end.

If you begin with ***Wrightslaw: Special Education Legal Developments and Cases 2015,*** you will see splits between the Circuits developing on two issues that later were addressed by the U.S. Supreme Court (SCOTUS) in the ***Fry*** and ***Endrew F.*** cases in 2017.

As you progress to the third book, ***Wrightslaw: Special Education Legal Developments and Cases 2017,*** you will read the decisions in ***Fry*** and ***Endrew F.*** and the transcripts of the remarks by Justice Kagan and Chief Justice Roberts.

These two unanimous pro-child decisions issued in early 2017 impacted numerous decisions the rest of that year and continuing through the present.

In ***Wrightslaw: Special Education Legal Developments and Cases 2017*** and ***Wrightslaw: Special Education Legal Developments and Cases 2018,*** you will see how some Circuits quickly issued decisions that put them in accord with the decisions by SCOTUS.

For example, one week after SCOTUS issued their unanimous decision in ***Endrew F.***, the Ninth Circuit issued a decision in the ***Antelope Valley*** case, one of our all-time favorites. The Ninth Circuit used the word "potential" when discussing an Individualized Education Program (IEP) and determining if the school provided a free appropriate public education (FAPE) to the child. You must consider the child's potential.

Other Circuits distinguished their decisions by explaining that the SCOTUS decision did not apply to the present case because the facts in the present case were unique and the SCOTUS ruling was not applicable.

As you read ***Wrightslaw: Special Education Legal Developments and Cases 2019,*** think about how a Court might rule on an issue. By learning the legal history of an issue, such as exhaustion, bullying, methodology, eligibility, etc., your ability to predict the outcome of future cases will be enhanced.

Sometimes you may hear someone complain about how special education law is always changing. Since 2004, there have only been a few changes in IDEA, the special education statute. Neither the statute nor the regulations are "always changing." However, new cases are issued regularly. For example, the important critical concept known as "compensatory education" that may impact COVID special education issues, has had major changes over several decades, even though that concept is not addressed in either the statute or regulations. It is strictly a creature of case law. See the compensatory education page on our website.

You may feel a sense of wonder as case law evolves and changes.

Strategies to Help You Use this Book

Hyperlinks

The e-book edition of ***Wrightslaw: Special Education Legal Developments and Cases 2019*** is an Adobe Portable Document File (PDF) with hyperlinks.

The first case in the Table of Cases (Chapter 4) and the Discussion of Cases (Chapter 5), is the January 3, 2019 decision by the Eighth Circuit - ***Dougherty v. Palmyra.*** **Click here for Chapter 4,** the Table of Cases and the ***Dougherty*** case and **click here for Chapter 5** and the discussion about the case.

As you move your cursor over a hyperlink, the **cursor will change its shape and become a hand** which means that those words are a hyperlink.

From the Table of Cases in Chapter 4, you can click on the ***Dougherty*** case name and you will then go directly to that case in this book in Chapter 5.

At the end of each case is a notation "**Return to Table of Cases**" which is also hyperlinked and will take you back to the Table of Cases.

Some URLs in the book are hyperlinks to other documents such as Federal Court Complaints, Jury Instructions, and Pleadings located on our www.wrightslaw.com website.

Search/ Find Feature

If you are looking for a specific case or concept, use the "Search/Find" feature in this e-book. To activate the Search/Find feature, press your "Control" or "Command" button and the letter "f " so a dialogue box pops up. The "Search/Find" feature is a fast, easy way to find information you need.

Index

The page numbers in the Index at the end of this book are hyperlinked to the referenced page. This **Index is atypical** because the page reference number does not take you to the indexed word in the case, but instead to **the beginning of the case** that contains that indexed entry.

In Summation

In the Introduction, you learned how ***Wrightslaw: Special Education Legal Developments and Cases 2019*** is organized and strategies to help you use this book.

You learned how you can develop expertise in special education law by reading cases from the U.S. District Courts and Courts of Appeal and how the books from the ***Wrightslaw: Special Education Legal Developments and Cases*** series can help in your quest.

It's time to move on to Chapter 1.

Chapter 1. Legal Concepts and Education Laws

In this chapter, you will learn about the four types of law with an overview of the federal laws that govern the education of children with disabilities. These federal education laws[2] include:

- Individuals with Disabilities Education Act (IDEA),[3]
- Section 504 of the Rehabilitation Act (Section 504),[4]
- Americans with Disabilities Act Amendment Act (ADA AA),[5]
- Every Student Succeeds Act (ESSA), [6]
- Fam ily Educational Rights and Privacy Act (FERPA),[7] and
- McKinney-Vento Homeless Assistance Act.[8]

Types of Law

There are four types of law: federal and state constitutions, statutes, regulations, and case law.

Case law refers to judicial interpretations of statutes and regulations that cause law to evolve and change. The essence of this book is focused on case law generated by the U.S. Courts of Appeal, the Courts that are one step below the U.S. Supreme Court.

Constitutional Law

The United States Constitution outlines the structure of the federal government. All laws passed must agree with the principles and rights set forth in the Constitution.

Article VI of the Constitution[9] includes the "**Supremacy Clause**." Pursuant to **Article VI** of the U.S. Constitution "the laws of the United States . . . shall be the **supreme law of the land**; and the judges in every state shall be bound thereby, anything in the . . . laws of any State to the contrary notwithstanding."

If a federal regulation or state law or regulation are in direct conflict with the United States Code (USC), the federal law controls. For that reason, it is important that you understand the federal law on an issue. If

2 References to the United States Code for each statute are provided below and hyperlinked.
3 20 USC § 1400, *et seq.* - https://www.law.cornell.edu/uscode/text/20/chapter-33
4 29 USC § 794, *et seq.* - https://www.law.cornell.edu/uscode/text/29/794
5 42 USC § 12101, *et seq.* - https://www.law.cornell.edu/uscode/text/42/12101
6 20 USC § 6301, *et seq.* - https://www.law.cornell.edu/uscode/text/20/6301
7 20 USC § 1232g - https://www.law.cornell.edu/uscode/text/20/1232g
8 42 USC § 11301, *et seq.* - https://www.law.cornell.edu/uscode/text/42/11301
9 https://www.law.cornell.edu/constitution/articlevi

there is a dispute and subsequent litigation, the USC is the law for federal judges and not state regulations. On occasion someone might tell you that, in their school district, they only follow the state regulations and not the federal law. That person does not understand that the federal law controls, not the state regulation. Most often however, on any particular issue, if you compare the state regulation to the federal law, it is often copy-paste verbatim text of the federal statute or federal regulation.

The first ten amendments to the Constitution[10] are the **Bill of Rights**. The Bill of Rights[11] is the source of the most fundamental rights – freedom of speech and religion, protection against unreasonable searches and seizures, and protection from cruel and unusual punishment.

The Fourteenth Amendment, added later, is titled "Civil Rights," but is better known as the "**Equal Protection Clause**." This Amendment and its sections were added to the Constitution to protect citizens against interference from the federal government.

Federal Statutes

Once a Bill is passed, Congress publishes the law as an "Act" in the Statutes at Large. That Act is then placed into the United States Code (USC) which is organized by subject. Most of the federal education laws are in Title 20 of the USC. The numbering system used to categorize an Act in the Statutes at Large is different from the system used in the United States Code. For example, if you are reading an article about IEPs and the author refers to it as being in Section 614 "of the Act," then you know the person was referring to the law before it was included in the United States Code. In the Code, the IEP statute is at 20 USC § 1414(d). In your writings, whether letters, briefs, or "scholarly" articles, you want to use the Code as your cited reference and not the Act. The United States Code is what Judges rely on when writing their decisions. The words in "The Act" are the same as the words in the Code, so cite the USC, but be aware that the numbers are different.

The United States Code has many subject classifications called Titles. Title 20 is about Education, Title 26 is the Internal Revenue Code, and Title 42 is about Public Health and Welfare. In each title, laws are indexed and assigned section numbers. The Individuals with Disabilities Education Act is cited as 20 USC § 1400, *et seq.* You will see some legal decisions and some articles reference the United States Code as USC, US Code, USCA, and USCS, with or without periods. The United States Code Annotated is the federal code in the book published by West Publishing. The United States Code Service is published by Lexis-Nexis. There does not appear to be a hard and fast rule whether or not to include periods in the letters referencing the federal code or even the federal regulations published in the Code of Federal Regulations (CFR).

Statutes are laws passed by federal, state, and local legislatures. In special education jargon, a reference to the "Code," is usually a reference to the Individuals with Disabilities Education Act, known as IDEA, which is located in the USC in Title 20 of Section 1400 and cited as 20 USC § 1400. The last substantial revision was in 2004, so this law is often referred to as "IDEA 2004" to differentiate it from the former version issued in 1997, known as "IDEA 97."

In addition to the IDEA, the two other federal statutes that directly affect the education of children with disabilities are Section 504 of the Rehabilitation Act, which begins at 29 USC § 794 *et seq.* and The Americans with Disabilities Act Amendments Act of 2008, known as ADA AA and as ADA, which begins at 42 USC § 12101, *et seq.*

10 https://www.law.cornell.edu/constitution
11 https://www.law.cornell.edu/constitution/billofrights

Individuals with Disabilities Education Act (IDEA 2004)

The most important statute in IDEA is the "Purposes" of the law, which is located in Section 1400(d). The statement of Purposes is your mission statement. The **primary purposes of IDEA** are:

> "[To] ensure that all children with disabilities have available to them a free appropriate public education that emphasizes special education and related services designed to meet their unique needs and prepare them for further education, employment and independent living . . . [and] to ensure that the rights of children with disabilities and parents of such children are protected . . ." **20 USC § 1400(d)** / Regulations at **34 CFR Part 300**

Section 1401 of IDEA includes thirty-six legal definitions in alphabetical order. Read the definitions carefully, especially the definitions of child with a disability, FAPE, related services, special education, supplementary aids and services, and transition services. At **34 CFR § 300.8**, the federal regulations published by the U.S. Department of Education provide more detail and specificity in regard to the definition of a child with a disability.

Section 1412 is about state responsibilities and includes least restrictive environment, child find, equitable services for children in private schools, unilateral placements, tuition reimbursement, and prohibitions on mandatory medication.

Section 1414 is about initial evaluations, eligibility for services, re-evaluations, and IEPs.

Section 1415 has prior written notice, the rules of procedure relating to mediation, due process hearings, court procedures, discipline, and exhaustion of administrative remedies.

Section 504 of the Rehabilitation Act of 1973

Section 504 of the Rehabilitation Act is a civil rights law that prohibits discrimination against individuals with disabilities. Title II prohibits discrimination on the basis of disability by state and local governments.

Section 504 is intended to ensure that children with disabilities have equal access to education. The purposes of Section 504 are:

> "To empower individuals with disabilities to maximize employment, economic self-sufficiency, independence, and inclusion and integration into society . . ." **29 USC § 701(b)**
>
> "No otherwise qualified individual with a disability in the United States . . . shall, solely by reason of her or his disability, be excluded from the participation in, be denied the benefits of, or be subjected to discrimination under any program or activity receiving Federal financial assistance . . ." **29 USC § 794** / Regulations at **34 CFR Part 104**

IDEA vis à vis Section 504

A child with a disability is entitled to a **Free Appropriate Public Education, known as FAPE**. However, there are significant differences between a FAPE under IDEA vis-à-vis Section 504.

Under IDEA, the initial FAPE statute is in the **definitions at 20 USC § 1401(9)**. FAPE under IDEA, requires the school to provide an Individualized Education Program (IEP) that is designed to meet the child's unique needs and provide the child with educational benefit. It was the subject of and defined in the SCOTUS 2017 *Endrew F.* case discussed in this book.

Under Section 504, FAPE is located in the **Regulations at 34 CFR § 104.33.** FAPE under Section 504 requires the school to provide regular or special education aids and services that meet the child's educational needs as adequately as the needs of non-disabled students are met.

With exceptions related to discipline and behavior issues, children and parents have fewer procedural protections under Section 504 than under the IDEA. However, under Section 504 parents can sue for dollar damages and obtain jury trials that are not available with IDEA cases. IDEA includes an elaborate system of procedural safeguards designed to protect the child and parents. These safeguards include written notice before any change of placement and the right to an independent educational evaluation at public expense. Section 504 does not include these protections.

Americans with Disabilities Act Amendments Act (ADA AA)

Congress amended the Americans with Disabilities Act (ADA) in 2008. It is known as both "ADA" and "ADA AA" the latter "AA" referring to "Amendments Act." In 2008, the amendments to ADA broadened the definition of disability. **Section 504 incorporates ADA requirements by reference and applies to all students who attend public schools.** Title II of the ADA applies to public schools and Title III to private schools, day care, and other entities open to the public. While the IDEA no longer applies when a student graduates from high school or ages out, Section 504 accommodations remain available to a student at a college or university.

Title II of the ADA states:

> "No qualified individual with a disability shall, by reason of such disability, be excluded from participation in or be denied the benefits of the services, programs, or activities of a public entity, or be subjected to discrimination by any such entity." **(42 USC § 12131 / Regulations at 28 CFR Part 35)**

Title III of the ADA states:

> "No individual shall be discriminated against on the basis of disability in the full and equal enjoyment of the goods, services, facilities, privileges, advantages, or accommodations of any place of public accommodation by any person who owns, leases (or leases to), or operates a place of public accommodation." **(42 USC § 12181, 12182 / Regulations at 28 CFR Part 36)**

Federal Regulations

After Congress reauthorized IDEA in 2004, the U.S. Department of Education (USDOE) developed and published proposed regulations in the Federal Register (FR), soliciting comments from citizens and stakeholders.

On August 14, 2006, the final IDEA 2004 Regulations and an "Analysis of Comments and Changes" (known as the "**Commentary**") were published in the FR. The "Commentary" includes questions from the public and the USDOE's answers. The full text and specific portions of the Commentary, including the Commentary about IEPs, is located in the IDEA 2004 section of the Law Library on the Wrightslaw.com site. (**Commentary, click here.**)

The IDEA 2004 Regulations are published in Volume 34, Part 300 of the Code of Federal Regulations (CFR). The legal citation for the regulations is **34 CFR Part 300 (hyperlink here).** Regulations must be consistent with the federal statute. They have the "force of law." Regulations may provide more details and specifics than the statute.

Our book, ***Wrightslaw: Special Education Law, 2nd Ed.*** contains the full text of the statute, i.e., IDEA 2004, and its federal regulations. It also includes portions of the other federal statutes listed above.

State Law and Regulations

State constitutions establish the structure of state governments. To receive federal special education funds, states must develop special education statutes and regulations that are consistent with the USC and the CFR.

State statutes and regulations may provide more rights than federal law but, pursuant to the Supremacy Clause, may not take away rights provided by federal law. When trying to find the answer to a legal question, begin with IDEA 2004, then look at the corresponding federal regulation.

After you understand the federal law and regulation, read your state special education law and regulation. In many cases, you will see that your state laws and regulations are a verbatim "copy and paste" of the federal law—but not always. Note any differences between federal and state law. Most states have very few special education statutes, with the bulk of state law contained in the state regulations.

Evolving Case Law & Legal Interpretations

Case Law

As you read the cases in this book, you will see inconsistencies from one court to another. You will also see how an issue, like "Exhaustion," also known as "Exhaustion of Administrative Remedies," evolves from decisions issued just a few years ago, like the 2017 SCOTUS *Fry* decision.

Legal Interpretations

Law is subject to different interpretations. As mentioned earlier, if you read an article about a special education case, the interpretations and conclusions in that article will reflect the opinions and biases of the author. If you read the case on your own, your interpretations and conclusions about the case may be quite different. This is why it is so important for you to read cases, statutes, and regulations yourself, instead of relying on the opinions of others.

When a case has compelling facts, the judge(s) may write a decision that is contrary to the current case law in that Circuit. To support this decision, the judge may find and use unique facts within the case or find a loophole in the law to create an "exception to the general rule." Decisions that are "exceptions to the general rule" cause that body of law to change and grow.

When Congress wants to pass a law but cannot agree on the precise wording of the proposed statute, members often compromise by using vague language in the bill. Vague words and phrases in statutes are confusing but are normal in all laws.

Assume you are researching a legal issue and find a U.S. Court of Appeals decision directly "on point." You will want to read the earlier U.S. District Court decision that triggered the appeal. When you read the earlier decision, you will have a clearer sense about other, factors and issues that may have affected the decision. You will also see how the law on this issue is evolving in your Circuit. As you read decisions from other Circuits, you will be in a stronger position to understand the evolution of the legal issue.

While one circuit takes a position that a specific law or statute is clear, another court may interpret the same law or statute differently and arrive at a different opinion. This is the nature of law.

Legal Citations - U.S.C. / F.3d

References to law are called legal citations. Legal citations are standardized formats that describe where you find a statute, regulation, or case. When you see a legal citation such as 20 USC § 1400 *et seq.*, the term "*et seq.*" means beginning in Volume 20 of the United States Code at Section 1400 and continuing thereafter. [**Wrightslaw Note**: It is usually italicized and there is never a period after the et, but always one after the seq.]

In the United States Code, the "Findings and Purposes" of the Individuals with Disabilities Education Act (IDEA) are in Section 1400 of Title 20. The legal citation for Findings and Purposes is 20 USC § 1400. You may refer to Findings and Purposes as "20 USC § 1400" or simply as "Section 1400."

Most federal courts of appeal and district court legal decisions are not published.

SCOTUS cases are published in U.S. Reports. The citation is the volume number, then "U.S." followed by the page number and year in parentheses. For example, this author's 1993 *Carter* case was published in Volume 510 of the U.S. Reports and it begins on page 7, thus the citation is 510 U.S. 7 (1993).

Published cases from the Courts of Appeal are located in the Federal Reporter, Third Series. They are cited as volume number, "F.3d," page number, and, in parentheses, the circuit and year. The *Carter* decision from the Fourth Circuit is cited as 950 F.2d 156 (4th Cir. 1991).

Courts of Appeal decisions from 1825 to 1925 are cited as volume number, "F." and page number, because they were in the first series of the Federal Reporter. Decisions issued in the second series between 1925 and 1993 were published in F.2d. In 1993, the third series of the Federal Reporter was published and is cited as F.3d. The volume number for F.3d has now passed 950. After publication of 999 F.3d, expected to be in the year 2025, legal citations will change to the Fourth Edition, i.e., F.4th.

For this author's *Carter* case, the District Court decision was not published in the Federal Reporter, but was published in the "Education for the Handicapped Law Reporter in volume 17 at page 452 and is thus cited as 17 EHLR 452.

Published District Court cases are in the Federal Supplement, Third Series. They are cited as volume number, "F. Supp.3d" page number, and, in parentheses, the district in that state, an abbreviation for that state followed by the year. For example, a 2020 case from a federal court in the Eastern District of Virginia could be cited as 123 F. Supp. 3d 456 (E.D. Va. 2020).

This book contains nearly every decision related to a special education legal case issued by U.S. Courts of Appeal in 2019.

We excluded a few decisions that were very short, usually one-page, and the decision did not include information of substance about the facts and legal issues in the case. We included the *Fry* case after remand to the U.S. District Court; a California state court case of significance; and two other District Court cases about private entities and ADA.

If you use Google Scholar and read the full text of some of these cases, you may notice a statement at the beginning: "Not Precedential" or "Do Not Publish" or "Not for Publication." This does not mean you cannot copy, print or rely on the decision in your case. Unless a decision includes other restrictions, "Do Not Publish" usually means that the judges on that panel think the decision is not noteworthy, does not create new legal precedent, and should not be published in the Federal Reporter.

The notation "Do Not Publish" is addressed in Rule 32.1, "Citing Judicial Dispositions," in the Federal Rules of Appellate Procedure (FRAP 32.1).

Fourteen of the cases in this book were published in the Federal Reporter, Third Edition, so there is no "F.3d" legal citation for most cases. A few cases in this book that do not currently have a F.3d citation may be published in F.3d later.

All Court of Appeals cases in this book are available from Google Scholar, a publicly accessible electronic database. All these cases can be shared and disseminated. Some of the referenced decisions also include information from the District Court. In most instances that information is available from Google Scholar. In some occasions and in order to obtain the Complaints, Jury Instructions and Jury Verdicts, we use the "**Public Access to Court Electronic Records (PACER)**" It is an electronic public access service that, for a fee, allows users to obtain case and docket information online from U.S. Courts of Appeal and U.S. District Courts.

In this chapter, you learned that statutes and regulations are not the same thing. In special education and disability law, the federal law is supreme, pursuant to the Supremacy Clause of the United States Constitution. It is important to always understand what the United States Code says on an issue. Next focus on the federal regulations and look at the case law from the U.S. Courts of Appeal. On any particular issue of importance, you will also want to look at decisions from your local District Court and state court, and your state statute and state regulations.

As a result of the two 2017 SCOTUS cases, *Fry* exhaustion of administrative remedies and *Endrew F.*'s definition of FAPE, what was the law was a few years ago, is different today. Law is always evolving.

Acronyms

In the Table of Cases, and the Cases themselves, you will see a number of acronyms. Frequent acronyms used are below:

ALJ	Administrative Law Judge	IEP	Individual Education Program
ARD	Admission, Review, Dismissal	IHO	Independent Hearing Officer
BIP	Behavioral Intervention Plan	LRE	Least Restrictive Environment
ESR	Evaluation, Summary, Report	RO	Review Office
FBA	Functional Behavioral Assessment	SCOTUS	Supreme Court of the US
FIE	Full and Individual Evaluation	SEHO	Special Education Hng Officer
HO	Hearing Officer	SLRO	State Level Review Officer
IEE	Independent Educational Evaluation	SRO	State Review Officer

It's time to move on to Chapter 2 to learn about the legal process and steps to resolve special disputes.

This page intentionally left blank.

Chapter 2

The Process to Resolve Special Education Disputes

The primary disputes between parents of children with special education needs and school districts concern issues related to a child's eligibility for services, content and implementation of the IEP, reimbursement for tuition in a private program or school, discipline, and allegations related to bullying and abuse.

There are several methods to resolve disputes between parents and school districts.[12] One, involving litigation, requires the filing of a request for a due process hearing against the school district. Other ways to resolve disputes include mediation or filing an administrative complaint with the state department of education or a federal agency such as the Office of Civil Rights or Department of Justice. Mediation is in the IDEA statute at 20 USC § 1415(e) and the IDEA State Administrative Complaint process is in the Code of Federal Regulations at 34 CFR § 300.153.

Special Education Due Process Hearings

If you become a party in a special education due process hearing, you must familiarize yourself with **20 USC § 1415** of IDEA. You must also learn about the federal special education regulations governing due process hearings contained in the Code of Federal Regulations (CFR), titled "Due Process Procedures for Parents and Children" (**34 CFR Part 300, Subpart** E).

Wrightslaw: Special Education Law, 2nd Ed., contains the complete statute, i.e., IDEA 2004 and all federal regulations. The statute that governs due process is at 20 USC § 1415 and begins on page 107 of the book. The regulations governing due process are at 34 CFR § 300.500, beginning on page 251.

In addition to becoming familiar with the federal statute and regulations, you must also be familiar with your state's statutes and regulations about due process hearings. You can locate your state's laws about special education by "Googling" the phrase "Yourstatename special education laws rules regulations." In most cases, the first suggested link will take you to your state's page that provides the complete regulations.

Your state's statute and regulations give the title of the individual who conducts hearings, listens to the evidence, and issues a ruling. In most states, this individual is called a Hearing Officer (HO), Independent Hearing Officer, Impartial Hearing Officer, Initial Hearing Officer (IHO), or Special Education Hearing

12 See ***Wrightslaw: All About IEPs***, Chapter 14. Resolving Parent-School Disputes, page 119.

Officer (SEHO). In a few states, this individual is known as an Administrative Law Judge (ALJ).

Your state statute and regulations describe the process you must follow to initiate a due process hearing. This usually requires filing a complaint with your State Department of Education (DOE) or, in some instances, with the State's Office of Administrative Hearings (OAH).

The rules and regulations governing when, where, and how to file the Due Process Complaint Notice, other procedural matters, appellate procedures, and timelines, vary from state to state. Failure to file the required documents, claims or missing deadlines may result in dismissal of the case.

After the Complainant, who most often is the parent, files the Due Process Complaint Notice (20 USC § 1415(c)(2)(A) - ***Wrightslaw***, page 109), the other party, often called the Respondent, pursuant to subsection (B) must file "a response that specifically addresses the issues raised in the complaint."

Once a due process complaint is filed, the Local Educational Agency (LEA) must convene a Resolution Session (20 USC § 1415(f)(1)(B) - ***Wrightslaw***, page 113) to provide the parties an opportunity to resolve their complaint before the due process hearing goes forward. The parents may waive the Resolution Session.

The special education due process hearing essentially is a trial including lay and expert witnesses, exhibits, testimony, and briefs filed by the parties. Schools are almost always represented by an attorney. Parents can retain an attorney or represent themselves. This self-representation is known as "pro se." In some states, parents can utilize the services of a "lay advocate" to represent them. In most states, unless permitted by state statute or regulation, this constitutes the unauthorized practice of law.

The losing party has the right to appeal a final due process decision. In most states, the losing party at a due process hearing appeals directly to either state or federal court. Those states with direct appeals to court are known as "Single-Tier States." The federal court is known as the U.S. District Court.

In a few states, including Kansas, New York, North Carolina, Ohio, Oklahoma, and South Carolina, an appeal is made to the State Department of Education for appointment of a Reviewing Officer (RO), State Review Officer (SRO), or a Review Panel. States with this second appellate level are known as "Two-Tier States." The losing party at the review level can then appeal directly to either state or federal court.

Appeal to the U.S. District Court

Most special education due process appeals to court are filed in a U.S. District Court, not in a state court.

If a special education due process hearing appeal filed in state court has a "Federal Question" as a possible issue, such as whether the IEP, as defined in federal law, i.e., 20 USC § 1414(d) (***Wrightslaw***, page 99) provides the child with FAPE, then, as a matter of right, pursuant to 28 USC § 1441(c), the other party can "remove" the case directly to federal court, i.e., the U.S. District Court. Special education cases typically have a "Federal Question." However, district courts must narrowly interpret the removal statute. There is a strong presumption that the case should stay in state court, especially if the plaintiff only alleged violations of rights guaranteed in the state's statute or constitution.

Typically, the complete lower level hearing record, including transcripts, exhibits, decisions, and briefs is filed with the U.S. District Court. The party appealing the case initiates this process by filing a "Complaint" which provides the factual and legal history of the case, and the legal basis for the desired relief. The other party files a responsive pleading, which might be an "Answer" or a "Motion to Dismiss," "Motion for Summary Judgment" or another pleading. These procedures are governed by the Federal Rules of Civil Procedure (Fed. R. Civ. P. / FRCP) (link here) and by that particular U.S. District Court's Local Rules of Practice.

At the district court level, depending on local rules of practice and caseload, the U.S. District Court Judge may assign the case to a federal Magistrate Judge who essentially acts in the capacity of the U.S. District Court Judge. The judge, whether a Magistrate Judge or full U.S. District Court Judge, rarely receives new evidence about the case. Instead, the judge generally reviews the lower level decision, the exhibits, the trial transcripts, and sometimes the pleadings previously filed in the case.

Motions for Judgment on the Administrative Record or Motions for Summary Judgment, frequently are filed by one or both parties. The decision issued by that federal judge usually will explain the legal process, discuss the Motions filed by the parties, the standards for reviewing the Motions, summarize each party's argument, give the legal and factual background of the case, and state the reasons justifying the final decision.

After the U.S. District Court has issued its final ruling, the losing party can appeal the case to the U.S. Court of Appeals for that Circuit.

Appeal to the U.S. Courts of Appeal

The U.S. Courts of Appeal consists of thirteen Circuits around the country. Each Circuit includes several states. (Table 1 below) Cases before the U.S. Courts of Appeal are heard by three Circuit Court Judges. In some instances, one sitting Judge might be a U.S. District Court Judge or a retired U.S. Supreme Court Justice. [In this author's ***Florence County School Dist. IV v. Shannon Carter***'s case when heard at the Fourth Circuit, retired U.S. Supreme Court Justice Lewis Powell was one of the three judges. In the decision, he wrote the portion about the split between Circuits and was present in the audience when this author argued the case before SCOTUS. Unanimous 9-0 ruling in our favor before SCOTUS in 1993. 510 US 7.][13]

Table 1. U.S. Courts of Appeal

Circuit	State	Circuit	States
1st	MA, ME, NH, RI, PR	7th	IL, IN, WI
2nd	CT, NY, VT	8th	AR, IA, MN, MO, ND, NE, SD
3rd	DE, NJ, PA, USVI	9th	AK, AZ, CA, GU, HI, ID, MT, NV, OR, WA
4th	MD, NC, SC, VA, WV	10th	CO, KS, NM, OK, UT, WY
5th	LA, MS, TX	11th	AL, FL, GA
6th	KY, MI, OH, TN	DC	Washington, DC

One appeals court is not included in Table 1. The Thirteenth Circuit, known as the "Federal Circuit," is not geographically based.

In the above Table, you will see that any case from a U.S. District Court in the state of New York must be filed in the U.S. Court of Appeals for the Second Circuit. Any case from a U.S. District Court in California must be filed in the U.S. Court of Appeals for the Ninth Circuit.

The Index at the end of this book includes a list of cases filed in the particular Courts of Appeal by Circuit number.

13 https://www.wrightslaw.com/law/caselaw/Carter_Links_Page.html

In 2019, the Ninth Circuit had sixteen cases, the Fifth Circuit had ten, and the Third Circuit had seven cases. The rest had five or less. There were nine cases from Texas (Fifth Circuit), eight cases from California, five from Hawaii, (both in the Ninth Circuit); and four from Massachusetts (First Circuit). Pennsylvania (Third Circuit) had four cases and Washington, DC had three cases. The remaining were two from Arkansas, Colorado, Florida, Kansas, Maryland, New York, and Virginia. There was one each from Arizona, Connecticut, Delaware, Kentucky, Maine, Ohio, Washington, and Wisconsin.

Filing and timeline rules for U.S. Courts of Appeal are provided in the Federal Rules of Appellate Procedure (**Fed. R. App. P. // FRAP) (link here**). Like due process regulations and the Federal Rules of Civil Procedure, one misstep, a failure to file within a specified timeline, or other error often is fatal to a case. When cases are submitted to the Courts of Appeal, no new evidence or testimony is submitted.

After Briefs and Oral Argument (if any), the Court of Appeals will issue a final ruling. This ruling may affirm i.e., uphold the ruling of the U.S. District Court, reverse the earlier ruling, or affirm some claims and reverse others. In some instances, the appellate court will remand all or part of the case back to the U.S. District Court for further evidence or determinations in light of the Circuit Court's ruling.

The Courts of Appeal typically have between one to two dozen Circuit Court judges appointed to hear appeals. A case is heard by a panel of three Judges in that Circuit. Pursuant to Federal Rule 35 of Appellate Procedure, [**FRAP 35, click here for hyperlink**], a losing party can file a petition requesting that all of the circuit judges in that court convene an "en banc" hearing and reverse the panel's decision. Such "en banc" rehearing petitions are rarely granted and reversals are rare.

A losing party can file a Petition for a Writ of Certiorari with the U.S. Supreme Court. This is a request for permission to appeal the case. "Of the 7,000 to 8,000 cert petitions filed each term, the court grants certiorari and hears oral argument in only about 80." [Source: https://www.scotusblog.com] Granting a cert petition requires the votes of four justices.

Appeal to the U.S. Supreme Court (SCOTUS)

The U.S. Supreme Court, often referred to in the legal community and in this book as "SCOTUS," accepts 100-150 of the more than 7,000 cases it is asked to review each year. Filing a Petition for a Writ of Certiorari is a request that SCOTUS accept the case. The Petition generally does not argue the nature of the alleged errors committed by the U.S. Court of Appeals, but instead argues why SCOTUS should decide to hear the case.

"A Petition for a Writ of Certiorari is rarely granted when the asserted error consists of erroneous factual findings or the misapplication of a properly stated rule of law." (**Rule 10 of the Rules of the Supreme Court of the United States.**)

Four of the nine Justices must vote to accept a case. Like the lower level courts, there are strict procedural rules which are **available online. (Click here.**)

The best route to SCOTUS accepting an appeal from the U.S. Courts of Appeal is when one circuit has issued a ruling that directly conflicts with a ruling from another circuit. This is known as a split between circuits.

When a federal judge in your state issues a decision that provides a new definition or legal standard, that decision is binding on the district courts in your state, but it is not binding on U.S. District Court judges in other states.

When a U.S. Court of Appeals issues a decision, that ruling is binding on all federal district courts within that circuit, but it is not binding on U.S. District Courts and U.S. Courts of Appeal in other parts of the country. That decision may, however, be considered "persuasive authority."

Split Between Circuits / U.S. Supreme Court

It is not unusual for one circuit to issue a ruling that is in direct conflict with another circuit, i.e., a "split between circuits." That's what happened in the author's ***Carter*** case.

In 1989, the U.S. Court of Appeals for the Second Circuit issued a decision in ***Tucker v. Bay Shore Union Free School Dist.***, 873 F.2d 563 (2d.1989). *Tucker* held that parents could not be reimbursed for private school tuition, even if the public school's IEP was not appropriate, if the private program was not on the state's approved list and the teachers were not certified or licensed by the state.

Later, in this author's case, ***Florence County Sch. Dist. IV v. Carter***, 510 U.S. 7 (1993), the Fourth Circuit held that reimbursement is proper if the private program is appropriate, even if the program is not on the state's approved list and the teachers are not certified by the state. The *Tucker* and *Carter* rulings were in conflict with each other and created a split between circuits.

In a landmark decision, SCOTUS unanimously upheld the Fourth Circuit's decision in *Carter*. This changed the legal landscape for tuition reimbursement cases, often known as *Carter* cases. The decision also opened the door for parents of children with autism to be reimbursed for expensive one-on-one ABA "Lovaas" therapy.

When the U.S. Supreme Court issues a ruling, pursuant to the Supremacy Clause of the U.S. Constitution, it becomes the "law of the land" and is binding throughout the country.

In ***Wrightslaw: Special Education Legal Developments and Cases 2015,*** we reported on decisions issued by the Sixth Circuit in the *Fry* case and by the Tenth Circuit in *Endrew F.*

In ***Wrightslaw: Special Education Legal Developments and Cases 2016***, we reviewed the issues in *Fry* and *Endrew F.* because SCOTUS had granted a Writ of Certiorari in both cases.

In ***Wrightslaw: Special Education Legal Developments and Cases 2017***, we included the full text of the decisions in *Fry v. Napoleon* and *Endrew F. v. Douglas County* that were issued by the U.S. Supreme Court in 2017. We included the transcript of remarks by Justice Kagan and Chief Justice Roberts when the Justices announced their decisions in these cases.

Wrightslaw: Special Education Legal Developments and Cases 2018 contained a number of Courts of Appeal cases that referenced those two cases issued by SCOTUS in 2017.

In this chapter you learned that if litigation occurs, there are clear legal and procedural steps that must be taken to resolve the dispute. If you become involved in litigation, assume that if you prevail, the opposition will appeal. If your case is sound, and you lose, you may have to appeal. In other words, be sure you understand the legal process and also assume that the case will go up on appeal, whether initiated by you or the opposition. Thus, at the initial stage, prepare the case for appeal.

Chapter 3

Finding Cases with Google Scholar

Legal Research - Google Scholar

Google Scholar (https://scholar.google.com/)is a free accessible search engine that indexes the full text of federal and state legal decisions. It allows you to search published opinions of state appellate and supreme courts since 1950, opinions from U.S. District Courts, U.S. Courts of Appeal since 1923, and decisions from the U.S. Supreme Court since 1791.

Google Scholar embeds clickable citation links within cases

As you locate and read a legal decision in Google Scholar, you will see references to earlier decisions within that same circuit, other circuits and even SCOTUS and district court cases. Those other case references are usually clickable links so that you can quickly jump to the case.

Google Scholar has a database about articles.

Another portion of Google Scholar searches peer-reviewed papers, theses, books, preprints, abstracts, and technical reports from academic publishers, professional societies, preprint repositories, universities, and scholarly articles available on the Internet.

Using Google Scholar

Go to: https://scholar.google.com/ and then click on "Case law" then "Select courts." In order to find all current U.S. District and Court of Appeals cases in a jurisdiction, for example, Virginia, related to IDEA, when the Courts page opens, go to the right column, "Federal courts," find Fourth Circuit, select the "Court of Appeals" for the 4th Circuit, and then select the ED and WD for Virginia, i.e., the Eastern and Western Districts, and then click "Done" at the bottom of that page.

A screen will open that instructs you to "Please enter a query in the search box above." Insert the following, word for word, with the quotation marks "individuals with disabilities education act" then add the current year such as 2020. Your search query will now read: "individuals with disabilities education act" 2020 (or the year you added). Hit return/enter on your keyboard and Google Scholar will do a full text search of all cases in their database from Court of Appeals for the Fourth Circuit and the Eastern and Western District federal district courts in Virginia. When the found cases are listed, there is a tab on that screen allows you to sort the cases, either by date issued or by relevance.

When you click on each of the case links, you will see the full text of the cases. To see cases for the prior year, go back to the "Query" screen and, in this instance, change the year to 2019 and resume the search. To find all cases in all of the District Courts in your circuit, go back to the "Select courts" screen and change your entry to the full circuit, and it will then show that you selected all of the states in the circuit. Then resume your search.

You can change your search query to look for cases that have other terms — dyslexia, autism, Section 504, restraint, damages, retaliation, "individualized educational program," "IEP," "independent educational evaluation," "IEE," "Americans with Disabilities Act," "compensatory education," etc. If your search term has two or more words, then you must use quotation marks around your search terms to avoid being flooded with cases that are not specific to your search but happen to have those words. For example, in the Fourth Circuit and its five states, if you simply search the phrase, Section 504, without quotations, Google Scholar will provide you with a listing of 7,020 cases. If you change the query to "Section 504" then the listing is reduced to 643 cases. If you add the number, 2020, to the query, you now have 14 cases listed in the Fourth Circuit and its five states of MD, NC, SC, VA, and WV.

When you change the selected courts to all federal and state courts around the country, you can broaden your search to find cases around the country. You can even search against the name of an individual, an administrator, an expert witness, a judge, or a school district.

Creating a Google Scholar Alert

Below the "Sort by date" tab is another that allows you to "Create alert." Whenever a new case comes out in those courts you selected with your search query, by entering your email address, you will receive an email from Google alerting you to the newly issued case with the link to open and read the case.

Troubleshooting

On occasion, you may search for a known case and not be able to find it. As we created the database of cases for our first 2015 book, we knew about a couple of decisions that did not appear when we used the query "Individuals with Disabilities Education Act" 2015. We were perplexed. We knew these cases existed but we could not find them in the Google database. When we experimented with different search terms, we found the cases. In one, the case had a hyphen and line break inside the word "education." In the decision it read as "Educa-tion" and thus the Google Scholar search engine did not find it.

Two cases from the Ninth Circuit referenced IDEA as the "Individuals with Disabilities Education Improvement Act." The word, "Improvement" caused the cases to be excluded in our initial search. When we changed our search term to "Individuals with Disabilities Education Improvement Act," we found the decisions. Another decision referred to IDEA as the Individual with Disability Education Act, i.e., individual was not plural and it used disability and not disabilities.

Given those differences, there is a definite possibility that there are some Courts of Appeal decisions in regard to IDEA that we do not know about and are not in this book.

In this chapter you learned how to find cases using any number of search terms using Google Scholar, a powerful tool.

Chapter 4
Table of Cases

Overview

This chapter includes a Table of Cases with all significant decisions in special education cases issued by the U.S. Courts of Appeal from January 1 through December 31, 2019. It includes a report from the U.S. Government Accountability Office (GAO) and three significant District Court cases, *Fry* and two ADA cases. One of the ADA cases involved a daycare center that was sued by the U.S. Department of Justice on behalf of a child with Down syndrome. In the other case, a medical student with dyslexia sued the National Board of Medical Examiners. [**Wrightslaw Note**: The U.S. District Court Complaints in each case are on our website and are hyperlinked in this book.]

In the Table, the first column is the date of the decision. The second column includes the Court of Appeals, the state where the case was litigated, and the name of the Judge who authored the opinion, if provided. In many cases, decisions are not written by a single judge, but by all three Judges on the panel, and thus no name is provided in the decision or in the Table.

The third column provides the abbreviated name of the case. Typically, names of the parties are abbreviated. Each case has a bookmark in the style (name) of the case. If you have the Adobe PDF edition of this book, when you click on the style of the case, you will be taken to the comprehensive summary of the case. If the case was published in F.3d, the citation is provided in that column just below the name of the case.

The fourth column describes key legal issues addressed in the ruling, outcome, and prevailing party.

Omissions, deletions, edits

Legal decisions contain numerous references to statutes, regulations, and other cases. These references, known as "citations," provide you with the specific legal authority, including the statute, i.e., United States Code (20 USC §1400), the federal special education regulation in the Code of Federal Regulations (34 CFR § 300.1), prior U.S. Court of Appeals decisions, and Opinions from the U.S. Supreme Court (SCOTUS). Citations within a decision may take up several lines of text. For reading clarity, in most instances we omitted these citations.

Courts of Appeal often quote other cases, testimony, and the exhibits used at trial. Typically, the Court will provide the source of that quote, which is often used with a quotation mark inside of a quotation mark such as " 'abc' ". However, again for visual and reading clarity, we deliberately omitted many single and double quotation marks, parentheses, brackets, other punctuation, and most legal citations. The text of some cases included obvious typographical, grammatical, and spelling mistakes. To make the decision easier to read and understand, we corrected those mistakes and purposely did not insert the usual and expected [*sic*] in the body of the quoted decision.

If you want to quote the legal language used by the Court in one of these cases, find the case in Google Scholar and use the exact language from the original decision issued by the Court. **Do not copy the text** in this book because of our omissions and edits explained in the above paragraph.

Table of Cases

Date	Circuit/State Author/Judge (if known)	Short Style F.3d Cite, if any	Description
1/3/2019	8th MO Stras	***Dougherty v. Palmyra Sch. Dist.*** 911 F. 3d 938	Even if parents opt out of IDEA services and do not want an IEP but only a Section 504 Plan, they must exhaust IDEA's administrative procedures in the event of a dispute about accommodations or services. **Outcome: School prevailed.**
1/15/2019	9th CA	***Solorio v. Clovis Unif. Sch. Dist.***	In this LRE case, the Court upheld the finding that the school's IEP was the LRE, relying on the *Rachel H.* factors. **Outcome: School prevailed.**
1/16/2019	5th TX Jones	***Renee J. v. Houston ISD*** 913 F. 3d 523	Seventeen year old child reads at the first grade level, IQ of 51, autism, ADHD and was not diagnosed until he was twelve. Did not receive services until he was fifteen, presented behavior problems, was bullied and absent for long periods of time. Parent requested a due process hearing alleging numerous violations and a denial of FAPE by the school district. The parents lost at due process, federal court, and before the Fifth Circuit. **Outcome: School prevailed.**
1/22/2019	7th WI Sykes	***P.F. v. Taylor, Supt DOE***	"Under Wisconsin's open-enrollment program, a public-school student can apply to transfer from his resident school district to a nonresident district that has an available space for him." Parents sued the State Superintendent of Instruction because placement decisions into an "open-enrollment" program were related to "the actual attributes of the child's handicap." Court of Appeals upheld the State's criteria. **Outcome: State DOE prevailed.**

Date	Circuit/State Author/Judge (if known)	Short Style F.3d Cite, if any	Description
1/24/2019	9th CA	***M.S. v. Los Angeles Unif. Sch. Dist.*** 913 F. 3d 1119	"The district court correctly concluded that M.S. was denied a FAPE because LAUSD was required to consider whether a residential placement should be offered to M.S. for educational purposes as part of her individualized education plan (IEP) notwithstanding that another county agency, the Department of Children and Family Services (DCFS), had residentially placed her for mental health treatment under state law, and pursuant to a Juvenile Court order." **Outcome: Parent prevailed.**
2/13/2019	3rd PA Porter	***Colonial School District v. G.K.***	This is an IEP lack of progress case. Parents prevailed at due process and District Court reversed explaining that the HO's post-IEP performance analysis was in error. The Circuit Court explained that the "Parents' claim that the IEP's goals were immeasurable was not a substantive error nor a procedural error that violated G.K.'s right to a free appropriate public education." **Outcome: School prevailed.**
2/13/2019	9th HI	***Ricks v. Hawaii State DOE***	In this case that went to a jury, the parent's lawsuit alleged that the use of a Rifton Chair violated Section 504. The verdict was in favor of the Hawaii State Dept. of Education. The parents appealed "the district court's rulings on evidence and the jury instructions" to the Ninth Circuit, which upheld the District Court. **Outcome: School prevailed.**
2/15/2019	1st ME Lynch	***Ms. S. v. Regional School Unit 72*** 916 F. 3d 41	In this statute of limitations case, it was asserted that Maine illegally reduced the SOL from four years to two years by failing to follow its own regulations regarding revisions. The District Court agreed and held in the instant case that the SOL was four years. The Court of Appeals reversed because "Maine intended to adopt a two-year limitations period that mirrors the IDEA's timing." **Outcome: School prevailed.**

Date	Circuit/State Author/Judge (if known)	Short Style F.3d Cite, if any	Description
2/25/2019	6th OH Kethledge	***Barney v. Akron Bd. Ed.***	"Delaina Barney argues that the Akron Board of Education violated the Individuals with Disabilities Education Act in nearly a dozen ways. The district court rejected all her arguments. We affirm." The parent made numerous allegations, many of which were disproved by her own testimony and exhibits. In a separate proceeding, discussed at the end of this case, attorney's fees were assessed against Barney's attorneys. **Outcome: School prevailed.**
3/5/2019	9th HI	***Oliver C. v. Hawaii DOE***	In this "stay-put" case, the Ninth Circuit explained that "We define 'current educational placement' as the placement set forth in the child's last implemented IEP. A change in location alone does not qualify as a change in 'educational placement.' Rather, a change in placement occurs when there is a significant change in the student's program. A change in location alone would not substantially or materially alter the child's educational program." The Court of Appeals upheld the Hearing Officer and District Court's finding that the physical move was not a change of placement triggering the stay-put statute. **Outcome: School prevailed.**
3/25/2019	4th MD Duncan	***R.F. v. Cecil County Public Schools*** 919 F. 3d 237	In this procedural violation case, the Fourth Circuit held that the school district's violation of IDEA "changing R.F.'s placement without involving them in an IEP meeting and by destroying data relating to R.F.'s progress on her IEP goals . . . neither constitutes a significant impediment to parental participation on these facts . . . those violations did not substantively deny R.F. a FAPE in violation of the IDEA." **Outcome: School prevailed.**

Date	Circuit/State Author/Judge (if known)	Short Style F.3d Cite, if any	Description
4/1/2019	5th TX	***E.M. v. Lewisville Indep. Sch. Dist.***	In this short, three paragraph opinion, the Fifth Circuit upheld the rulings by the ALJ and District Court in this speech impairment case. "In a detailed opinion, the district court concluded that E.M. had not and was unlikely to make meaningful progress in articulating sounds, did not use her sign language interpreter, and instead communicated primarily and relatively successfully through assistive technology . . . the challenged IEP was reasonably calculated to enable E.M. to receive educational benefits as required under the IDEA." **Outcome: School prevailed.**
4/12/2019	4th VA	***Lucas v. Henrico County Sch. Bd.***	This unusual case involved a parent and two lay advocates filing suit against the school district, school district staff, the police, the state court criminal prosecutor and the state court general district criminal court judge. The parent and advocates were arrested for trespassing at the public school, convicted, and filed suit in federal court alleging violations of IDEA, ADA, Section 504 and related state law claims. The district court dismissal of almost all claims was upheld by the Fourth Circuit. Since the criminal court convictions were still on appeal in state court, the District Court was premature with one issue and that issue was remanded. **Outcome: County prevailed.**
4/24/2019	9th CA	***Morales v. Newport-Mesa Unif. Sch. Dist.***	Halfway through her senior year, Morales "was hit by a car, resulting in life-threatening injuries and traumatic brain injury." After Morales graduated from high school, her mother requested a due process hearing against the school district. The Ninth Circuit explained that "The record supports the ALJ's determination that Morales's mother received the procedural safeguards required under 34 C.F.R. § 300.504, and that any other procedural violations of Morales's rights were harmless for the reasons identified by the ALJ. A procedural violation does not constitute a denial of a FAPE if the violation fails to result in a loss of educational opportunity." **Outcome: School prevailed.**

Date	Circuit/State Author/Judge (if known)	Short Style F.3d Cite, if any	Description
4/29/2019	9th CA	***R.M. v. Gilbert Unif. Sch. Dist.***	In this short, three paragraph decision, in regard to LRE, the *Rachel H.* case, and change of placement / location issues, the Ninth Circuit upheld the District Court's ruling that the child was provided FAPE in the least restrictive environment. "The student's academic needs weigh most heavily against a mainstream environment . . . [and] this proposal was a change in 'location' only." **Outcome: School prevailed.**
5/9/2019	9th HI	***J.B. v. Hawaii DOE***	This case concerns LRE, methodology and the child's transition from a small private school for students with autism into a Hawaii public school. Among the issues raised by the parent related to the DOE's failure to specify "the use of Applied Behavioral Analysis (ABA) methodology in J.B.'s IEP." The Ninth Circuit noted that "The principal and the teachers explained that they did not want to specify ABA methodology in the IEP because the teachers wanted to use more than one methodology . . . DOE was not required to specify ABA methodology in J.B.'s IEP." The Court stated that failure to specify a teaching methodology in the IEP is not a violation of IDEA. **Outcome: School prevailed.**
5/15/2019	5th TX Higginson	***Lisa M. v. Leander Indep. Sch. Dist.***	In this eligibility dispute, the Court noted that after initially finding the child eligible for an IEP, after a meeting with "outside counsel," the central office "District personnel at some level intervened with J.M.'s teachers, . . . either directing or training them to a finding of no eligibility in the February ARDC meeting." "The SEHO ordered the District to convene an ARD committee meeting and 'revise the existing IEP as was planned' for the February ARD committee meeting." SEHO, District Court and Court of Appeals all agreed that the child "needed" special education and thus was eligible. **Outcome: Parent prevailed.**

Date	Circuit/State Author/Judge (if known)	Short Style F.3d Cite, if any	Description
5/20/2019	CA State Court of Appeals Willhite	***B.H. v. Manhattan Beach Unif. Sch. Dist.*** 35 Cal. App. 5th 563	The adoptive parents of a former foster child placed their child into a facility outside of their home school district while utilizing some federal adoption assistance funding. The home school district refused to provide funding. This action was upheld by the hearing officer and a California state court judge. On appeal, the state appellate court discussed the purpose of the federal financial adoption assistance and explained that "the fundamental purpose of such legislation is the welfare of the children. The code must be interpreted reasonably and the court must maintain its focus on what benefits the student, not the school district." **Outcome: Parents prevailed.**
5/21/2019	DC Tatel	***D.L. v. District of Columbia***	This is a multi-million dollar attorney fee case where the requested $9.76 million fee was reduced to a $6.96 million award. It involves issues unique to the U.S. District Court in Washington D.C. and the "matrix" used to calculate fees. The DC Circuit Court explained that "as District counsel recognizes, that fees are lower in rural areas than in the District. Indeed, the District's own evidence shows that rates for legal services in the District of Columbia are among the highest anywhere." The reduced award was vacated and case remanded for the Court to re-evaluate fees. **Outcome: Parent's attorneys prevailed. Fee award to be recalculated.**
5/22/2019	1st MA	***C.D. v. Natick Pub. Sch. Dist.***	This tuition reimbursement case included issues related to mainstreaming and differing positions of other Courts of Appeal. The parents challenged "this circuit's prior interpretations of these IDEA requirements as incomplete or as inconsistent with the IDEA and current Supreme Court case law. The parents seek reimbursement for at least three years of C.D.'s education in a specialized private school." The Court discussed a number of the landmark LRE/Mainstreaming cases and concluded that the school's IEP was the LRE. **Outcome: School prevailed.**

Date	Circuit/State Author/Judge (if known)	Short Style F.3d Cite, if any	Description
5/24/2019	4th MD	***E.S. v. Smith + Montgomery County Pub. Sch.***	Parents alleged that the school's failure to include them in planning meetings in regard to the IEP constituted a violation of IDEA and denial of FAPE. The Fourth Circuit, relying on its earlier 2019 decision in *R.F. v. Cecil Cty. Pub. Schs.* did not agree because, even though a violation had occurred, it did not "significantly impede" the parents. **Outcome: School prevailed.**
5/31/2019	4th VA Diaz	***J.D. v. Colonial Williamsburg Fdtn.*** 925 F. 3d 663	This Colonial Williamsburg restaurant 504/ADA case involved a child allergic to gluten. Because of numerous prior adverse incidents, the child would not eat restaurant "gluten free" prepared food and instead brought his own homemade food. During a school field trip, the restaurant would not permit the child to eat the homemade food in the restaurant. Pursuant to a subsequent ADA lawsuit filed in federal court, the Court dismissed the case, family appealed, and the Fourth Circuit reversed and re-instated the request for a jury trial. **Outcome: Parent prevailed.**
6/4/2019	10th KS Lucero	***Donahue v. Kansas Bd. Ed.***	The pro se parent's request for a due process hearing was dismissed pursuant to a Notice of Insufficiency. The dismissal was upheld by a Review Officer. The parent appealed to the U.S. District Court, requested a preliminary injunction, and also "filed multiple lawsuits on the same subject matter." Named defendants were the Hearing Officer, the Review Officer, the Governor, "and officials of the Kansas Division of Child and Family Services (DCF), Danielle Bartelli (an officer of KVC, a company providing child welfare services), and Johnson County District Attorney Stephen Howe." A number of her pleadings were "untimely." The Court of Appeals upheld the dismissal. **Outcome: School prevailed.**

Date	Circuit/State Author/Judge (if known)	Short Style F.3d Cite, if any	Description
6/7/2019	9th CA	***E.B. v. Baldwin Park Unif. Sch. Dist.***	In this legal procedures case about judicial discretion, for reasons unrelated to this case, the parent's attorney was suspended by the State Bar. He arranged for a substitution of counsel which was denied by the District Court four months later. The Court, on its own motion, ordered the "case dismissed for lack of prosecution." Parents subsequently appealed to the Ninth Circuit which reversed, finding an abuse of discretion by the District Court. **Outcome: Parent prevailed.**
6/10/2019	6th KY Daughtrey	***L.G. v. Fayette County Bd. Ed.***	In this *Fry* "Exhaustion" case, the parent filed a lawsuit without requesting a special education due process hearing. The case was dismissed pursuant to the failure to exhaust. Because of medical advice related to an e-coli infection, the child was absent from school for an extended period of time. The school filed a truancy petition and a complaint with protective services. The parent filed suit alleging a violation of Section 504. Sixth Circuit upheld dismissal because the parent failed to exhaust. **Outcome: School prevailed.**
6/12/2019	8th AR Wollman	***Albright v. Mountain Home Sch. Dist.***	In this judicial discretion case the Court of Appeals noted "a long history of bad blood has accumulated between Ms. Albright and the District concerning Child Doe's educational needs. The due process complaint that is the subject of the instant appeal, for example, was actually the third such complaint that Ms. Albright filed against the District . . . [and then] Ms. Albright also filed three more due process complaints against the District." There were a number of late filings by her counsel in this and other cases and the District Court "denied Albright's out-of-time filing request, struck her filings from the record, and granted the District's motion for summary judgment." The Eighth Circuit upheld the dismissal because "her filing it ten days after the deadline did not create good cause where none previously existed." **Outcome: School prevailed.**

Date	Circuit/State Author/Judge (if known)	Short Style F.3d Cite, if any	Description
6/12/2019	9th CA	***C.Q. v. River Springs Charter Schools***	In this "stay-put," pendency case, the school intended to transfer a child to a different school during spring break of her current semester. The District Court Judge "conducted a de novo review of the issue and granted C.Q.'s motion. River Springs timely appealed" to the Ninth Circuit which upheld the District Court. **Outcome: Stay-put upheld, child prevailed.**
6/12/2019	10th CO Briscoe	***Steven R.F. v. Harrison Sch. Dist. No. 2***	In this tuition reimbursement case, the parent filed a state complaint, prevailed, and school district requested due process on the same issue and prevailed. On parent's appeal, the District Court reversed, ruled in the parents favor and entered an order for attorney's fees. The school district appealed to the Tenth Circuit. Pursuant to "stay-put," the school district continued to pay the private school tuition as the case was pending. The Tenth Circuit found that, since tuition had been paid, the case was now moot and vacated the District Court's decision in favor of parents. The entitlement to the attorney's fees were lost by the parent even though the parent prevailed at the prior level. [**Wrightslaw Note**: See the November 14, 2019 Tenth Circuit *Nathan M.* case. Same circuit, same issue, same result.] **Outcome: Parent prevailed, but case moot, no attorney's fees.**
6/14/2019	2nd NY Hall	***W.A. v. Hendrick Hudson Cent. Sch. Dist.***	This tuition reimbursement case involved four conflicting decisions by an IHO and SRO. The Court of Appeals explained that "If the SRO and IHO decisions conflict, the IHO's decision may be afforded diminished weight. In other words, we would defer to the final decision of the state authorities, that is, the SRO's decision. Yet such deference applies only to the SRO's reasoned conclusions . . . [if] inadequately reasoned, in which case a better-reasoned IHO opinion may be considered instead." **Outcome: School prevailed.**

Date	Circuit/State Author/Judge (if known)	Short Style F.3d Cite, if any	Description
6/20/2019	3rd NJ Matey	***M.G. v. North Hunter-don-Voorhees Reg. High Sch. Dist.***	Parent's emotionally charged, sarcastic, critical testimony was discredited and "not anchored on any competent evidence beyond personal experience . . . the District Court appropriately deferred to the ALJ's credibility determinations." The Court of Appeals affirmed the ALJ and District Court rulings that the school's proposed IEP was appropriate. **Outcome: School prevailed.**
6/26/2019	11th FL Gran	***L.J. v. Broward County Sch. Bd.***	The "child" was 26 years old. The Eleventh Circuit was distressed by the delayed decisions from the ALJ and District Court Judge. A "stay-put" IEP was in effect from the seventh grade. Parent attacked its implementation, not its content. "Confronting this issue for the first time ourselves, we conclude that to prevail in a failure-to-implement case, a plaintiff must demonstrate that the school has materially failed to implement a child's IEP." The Court found that there was not a material failure to implement the "stay-put" IEP. **Outcome: School prevailed.**
6/27/2019	9th HI	***J.G. v. Hawaii DOE***	In this relatively short opinion, the Ninth Circuit placed the burden of proof on the parents even though the school district sought to change the child's placement and prepared a new IEP. "The burden of proof in an administrative hearing challenging an IEP is properly placed upon the party seeking relief. In this case, that party is the student, as represented by his parents." **Outcome: Hawaii State DOE prevailed.**
7/1/2019	9th CA	***Jay F. v. Hart Sch. Dist.***	In this discipline/manifestation determination case, the Ninth Circuit vacated an agreement to expel the child and agreed with the District Court that the earlier adverse ruling by the ALJ was not thorough and careful. The Court affirmed the Order that, as compensatory education, the school district also had to provide "dialectical behavioral therapy as relief" for the district's violations. **Outcome: Student prevailed.**

Date	Circuit/State Author/Judge (if known)	Short Style F.3d Cite, if any	Description
7/2/2019	2nd NY	***R.H. v. Saugerties Cent. Sch. Dist.***	In this tuition reimbursement case, the IHO ruled in favor of the parents, the SRO reversed finding that there was insufficient evidence that the private school was appropriate. On appeal, both the District Court and Court of Appeals upheld the finding of the SRO. **Outcome: School prevailed.**
7/5/2019	DC Henderson	***Brown v. DCPS***	In this ten-year old class action case, the "unjustified segregation of disabled individuals in institutions is a form of disability discrimination." Pursuant to the SCOTUS *Olmstead* decision, Washington, D.C. must prove that it either has an "*Olmstead* Plan" in place or that the requested transfer of disabled individuals from nursing homes to community care would be costly and unreasonable. **Outcome: Individuals with disabilities prevailed.**
7/9/2019	10th KS Phillips	***Donahue v. Brownback (Gov, Kansas)***	Child was restrained at school "in a 5x4 isolation prison cell, located inside his autism classroom." Because of a state statute, signed by the Governor authorizing some forms of restraint, the parent, pro se, without benefit of counsel, sued the Governor. The case was dismissed by the District Court, upheld by the Court of Appeals noting that the Eleventh Amendment Immunity barred the official-capacity claims for monetary damages against the Governor. **Outcome: Kansas and the former Governor prevailed.**
7/10/2019	3rd DE Smith	***A.H. v. Colonial Sch. Dist.***	This is a reverse due process IEE case in which the parent requested an IEE more than a year after the initial evaluation. The school refused, requested a due process hearing against the family, and prevailed at each level. **Outcome: School prevailed**

Date	Circuit/State Author/Judge (if known)	Short Style F.3d Cite, if any	Description
7/17/2019	1st MA Lipez	***G. v. Fay Sch.***	Because the child allegedly suffered from a sensitivity to WiFi at the private school, which refused to remove the WiFi, a lawsuit was filed that alleged violation of ADA and also retaliation. It includes a discussion about the *Daubert* Rule and use of expert witnesses. The District Court dismissed the case, which was upheld by the First Circuit. **Outcome: School prevailed.**
7/18/2019	9th WA	***Edmonds Sch. Dist. v. A.T.***	This is a tuition reimbursement case in which the Ninth Circuit spelled out the required elements in the "two prong test" in order to award tuition as was upheld in this case. **Outcome: Student prevailed.**
7/19/2019	DC Millett	***M.K. v. El Haynes Charter Sch.***	"The district court in this case wrongly denied a stay-put injunction because it placed the burden of proof on the student rather than the local educational agency. And that error has continuing adverse consequences for the student's claim for compensatory education. The purpose of the stay-put command is to strip schools of the unilateral authority they traditionally employed to exclude disabled students from school." **Outcome: Case remanded, student prevailed.**
7/22/2019	3rd PA Scirica	***Anderson v. Abington Hgts. Sch. Dist.***	School failed to follow Section 504 discipline procedures when it expelled a Section 504 child for more than a year without either an IDEA manifestation hearing or Section 504 evaluation and hearing. School appealed adverse due process decision to federal court and the parties settled the case. Parents later filed a Section 504 lawsuit in federal court, which was dismissed. The Third Circuit found that the violations of the Section 504 procedures were "educational claims" fully litigated at the due process hearing, thus making the case "res judicata" and a part of the settlement agreement. **Outcome: School prevailed.**

Date	Circuit/State Author/Judge (if known)	Short Style F.3d Cite, if any	Description
7/25/2019	2nd CT Livingston	***P.J. v. Connecticut State BOE***	This is a class action least restrictive environment (LRE) attorney fee case that began in 1991, has had a "tortuous history," with a settlement agreement in March, 2002 that included $675.000 in fees and subsequent monitoring. In 2017, the plaintiffs "requested $906,010.85 in attorneys' fees and $197,181.15 in costs," but were only awarded $470,727.57. Connecticut appealed the entitlement to any fees, and the Second Circuit upheld the entitlement, but reduced some of the hours and remanded it back to the District Court for further calculations. **Outcome: Plaintiffs prevailed, partially, award reduced.**
7/25/2019	3rd PA Rendell	***LeJeune G. v. Khepera Charter Sch.***	In this case about appellate procedure, the parent sued the insolvent charter school and the PA DOE for previously agreed on payment for private school tuition. At District Court, the Parent lost the essence of the desired relief. On appeal to the Third Circuit, the parent changed the legal strategy/theory as to the basis for the payment. The Court of Appeals found the issue waived as it was not raised in the District Court. **Outcome: PA State DOE prevailed.**
8/6/2019	9th AZ	***Pangerl v. Peoria Unif. Sch. Dist***	This is an IEP parental participation and due process procedural timeline errors case. The school continued an IEP meeting for twenty additional minutes after the parents left the meeting. The Hearing Officer's decision was not issued until fourteen months after the due process complaint was filed. The District Court and Court of Appeals both held that the procedural violations did not result in loss of an educational opportunity. **Outcome: School prevailed.**

Date	Circuit/State Author/Judge (if known)	Short Style F.3d Cite, if any	Description
8/8/2019	1st MA Lynch	***Parent/Professional Advoc League, Disability Law Center, MW v. Springfield Pub. Sch.*** 934 F.3d 13	This *Fry* exhaustion case is about "standing" to bring a lawsuit, certification of a class, and the "overlap" between Title II of the ADA and the LRE requirements of IDEA. Springfield places 230 "students with mental health disabilities in a separate and inferior school, the Springfield Public Day School" and not in the LRE neighborhood school. The District Court dismissed the case finding that the two organizations did not have standing to bring the suit. Because this was an IDEA LRE claim, it should have been exhausted pursuant to *Fry*. District Court was upheld by Court of Appeals. **Outcome: School prevailed.**
8/8/2019	5th TX	***W.V. v. Copperas Cove Indep. Sch. Dist.***	In this eligibility determination case the District Court found that the child had dyslexia, but failed to make findings as to whether, because of the dyslexia, the child "by reason thereof, needs special education and related services" and was thus eligible for an IEP. Case vacated and remanded for the District Court to make the required findings. **Outcome: Neither party prevailed.**
8/12/2019	9th CA Schroeder	***Paul G. v. Monterey Peninsula Unif. Sch. Dist. + CA DOE*** 933 F.3d 1096	This is a *Fry* exhaustion case in which the school agreed to place the California child in a residential facility in Kansas. Paul was 18 at that time and no CA facility would accept him because of his age. Due process hearing sought against the school district and state department of education for failing to have an in-state residential facility available. Hearing officer dismissed the case against the state and "Paul then entered into a settlement agreement with the school district in which OAH dismissed the case without ever ruling on his claim that the lack of an in-state residential facility had denied him a FAPE." Subsequent suit against CA DOE was dismissed for failure to exhaust administrative remedies. **Outcome: CA State DOE prevailed.**

Date	Circuit/State Author/Judge (if known)	Short Style F.3d Cite, if any	Description
8/26/2019	1st MA Lipez	***Doucette v. Georgetown Pub. Sch.*** 936 F.3d 16	This is another *Fry* exhaustion case in which the facts are quite identical to those in the original *Fry* case. School would not let the service dog accompany the child, who subsequently suffered seizures and hospitalizations on several occasions. Parents removed the child from the public school, who then threatened the parents with charges of truancy. Court of Appeals reversed the District Court and held that exhaustion was not required. **Outcome: Parent prevailed.**
8/28/2019	5th TX Graves	***Wilson v. Southlake Police Dept.*** 936 F. 3d 326	In this Section 504 / ADA case, an eight year old child with autism had a melt down at school and was handcuffed by the School Resource Officer, who berated the child and later the parents. The SRO was not properly trained in how to handle such incidents. The District Court dismissed the case and the Court of Appeals re-instated it and remanded it back. **Outcome: Parent prevailed.**
9/16/2019	5th TX Brown	***Spring Ranch Indep. Sch. Dist. v. O.W.*** 938 F.3d 695	This is a child find, FAPE, tuition reimbursement and compensatory education case. The school violated child find because of its "continued use of behavioral interventions," violated the IEP by reducing the school day to three hours and the child was awarded compensatory education. **Outcome: Parent prevailed.**
9/17/2019	11th FL Boggs	***US v. Florida*** 938 F. 3d 1221	The Attorney General on behalf of the United States Department of Justice filed a lawsuit against Florida in regard to having unnecessarily institutionalized hundreds of children with disabilities in nursing facilities. Florida asserted that the Attorney General was not a "person" who could allege discrimination and thus did not have standing to sue. The District Court judge agreed and dismissed the case. The Eleventh Circuit reversed and held that the Attorney General did have standing. Case remanded back to the District Court. **Outcome: United States prevailed, however a Petition for a Rehearing is pending.**

Date	Circuit/State Author/Judge (if known)	Short Style F.3d Cite, if any	Description
9/25/2019	District Court MI Cox	***Fry v. Napoleon Comm. Sch.*** **(on remand to District Court from SCOTUS)**	The *Fry* exhaustion of administrative remedies case before the U.S. Supreme Court was remanded back to the U.S. District Court for a Jury Trial. This is the last Opinion and Order of substance issued by that District Court prior to the Pretrial Order issued a month later in preparations for the upcoming Jury Trial. (Links to case developments provided.) Case subsequently settled. **Outcome: Parent prevailed.**
10/2/2019	5th TX Costa	***McMillen v. New Caney Indep. Sch. Dist.***	In this failure to exhaust case, the child's behavior worsened in his junior year, the school changed his IEP and placed him with a teacher who "tried to 'save' McMillen . . . [by having him] take herbal supplements that she thought could cure his autism. She also tried to convert McMillen to Christianity, believing that if he converted his disabilities would be cured." Later, she turned on him and he was eventually arrested "and charged with the felony of making a terroristic threat." The felony charge was dropped in exchange for parents "agreeing to never return McMillen to the school district." Later lawsuit for damages was dismissed by District Court for failure to exhaust administrative remedies and upheld by Court of Appeals. **Outcome: School prevailed**
10/10/2019	5th TX	***A.B. v. Clear Creek Indep. Sch. Dist.***	This is an LRE case in which the school district proposed a change of placement, parents objected, requested a due process hearing, and prevailed before the Hearing Officer and District Court. On school's appeal to the Fifth Circuit, that Court, in ruling in the parent's favor, relied on the landmark 1989 *Daniel R.R.* case and explained that the "analysis goes beyond whether the student will gain any educational benefit from regular education because educational benefits are not mainstreaming's only virtue." **Outcome: Parents prevailed.**

Date	Circuit/State Author/Judge (if known)	Short Style F.3d Cite, if any	Description
10/25/2019	5th TX Haynes	***T.W. v. Dallas Indep. Sch. Dist.*** 941 F.3d 224	District Court twice dismissed a Title IX, sex discrimination claim of rape by a student on a special needs child because the parents failed to exhaust their administrative remedies. Pursuant to the Supreme Court's ruling in *Fry*, the Court of Appeals reversed and remanded the case back to the District Court. **Outcome: Parents and child prevailed.**
10/28/2019	9th HI	***Kimes v. Matayoshi, Hawaii Supt DOE***	This was an appeal from a four-day Section 504 jury trial related to discipline, restraints, reasonable accommodations and deliberate indifference in which the jury ruled against the parents. The parents requested that the District Court set aside the verdict as contrary to law, which he refused to do. On appeal, the Ninth Circuit explained the required standard to recover damages against the school district, noting that parents did not meet that requirement. **Outcome: School prevailed.**
10/29/2019	3rd PA Fisher	***Pocono Mtn. Sch. Dist. v. T.D.***	In this tuition reimbursement case, as the case was pending, the school district continued to pay the private school tuition. School appealed to the Third Circuit, which found the case to be moot since "neither party has a personal stake in the outcome of the claims related to tuition reimbursement." Parents did prevail on the award of 26 hours of compensatory education. **Outcome: Parent prevailed.**
11/4/2019	GAO	**GAO Report to Congress Dispute Resolution**	Government Accounting Office issued a report to Congress titled "***IDEA Dispute Resolution Activity in Selected States Varied Based on School Districts' Characteristics.***" "GAO reviewed publicly available data on dispute resolution at the state level and collected data at the school district level from five states—Massachusetts, Michigan, New Jersey, Ohio, and Pennsylvania—selected based on the number of disputes initiated and school district characteristics, among other factors."

Date	Circuit/State Author/Judge (if known)	Short Style F.3d Cite, if any	Description
11/13/2019	District Court NJ Hillman	***USA v. Nobel Learning***	The U.S. Department of Justice (USDOJ) sued the day-care Chesterbrook for violation of Title III of the ADA because the child with Down syndrome, after three years in the program, was not toilet trained and was subsequently expelled. Because of this violation of the ADA, Chesterbrook had to revise, publicize, and disseminate their non-discrimination policies and make monetary payments to the parents and the United States. **Outcome: Parents and USDOJ prevailed.**
11/14/2019	10th CO McHugh	***Nathan M. v. Harrison Sch. Dist.*** 942 F.3d 1034	This is another case becoming moot after the passage of time where the private school tuition continued to be paid by the school district as the litigation continued. Decision relied on the Tenth Circuit's earlier June 12, 2019 *Steven R.F. v. Harrison Sch. Dist.* case with similar facts. **Outcome: Neither prevailed, case dismissed as moot.**
12/17/2019	3rd NJ Matey	***Marlboro Bd. Ed. v. H.L.***	At a due process hearing for tuition reimbursement, prior to evidence being heard, the School Board filed a Motion to Dismiss asserting that parents failed to participate in a resolution session. The ALJ refused to dismiss at that early stage, school appealed to federal court which dismissed the school's case for failure to exhaust administrative remedies. School appealed to the Third Circuit which upheld District Court. **Outcome: Parents prevailed.**
12/17/2019	5th TX	***Bruno v. Northside Indep. Sch. Dist.***	In this "comparable IEP" case related to a child's move from Florida to Texas, the new school district completed new evaluations, changed his placement, and reduced the related services. Upheld by the Hearing Officer, District Court and Court of Appeals. **Outcome: School prevailed.**

Date	Circuit/State Author/Judge (if known)	Short Style F.3d Cite, if any	Description
12/20/2019	8th AR	***Wofford v. North Little Rock Sch. Dist.***	In this attorney fee case where parents prevailed at due process and a new IEP was ordered, they were denied attorneys' fees because they moved out of the District before the IEP meeting was completed. **Outcome: School prevailed.**
12/30/2019	PA District Court Joyner	***Ramsay v. NBME***	The National Board of Medical Examiners violated the ADA by refusing to provide the testing accommodations to the medical student that she had from her undergraduate years through medical school. **Outcome: Student prevailed.**
			End of Table of Cases

Return to the Top of the Table of Cases

Chapter Five beginning on the next page has the decisions issued by the Courts of Appeal and referenced in the above table.

Chapter 5
U.S. Court of Appeals Cases

Dougherty v. Palmyra Sch. Dist.
8th Circuit
911 F. 3d 938
Judge Stras
1/3/2019 - Missouri

In this *Fry* exhaustion case, where parents of a child with Down Syndrome refuse consent for services under IDEA, reject an IEP, and only want a Section 504 Plan that would have provided the educational accommodation of an iPad, can parents file suit without exhausting their administrative remedies? "At the heart of their lawsuit was the claim that, by failing to provide educational accommodations, Palmyra had denied E.D. access to a free public education."

"Before he began kindergarten at Palmyra Elementary School, his mother informed the school that she was seeking accommodations for his disability. E.D.'s parents had some specific accommodations in mind, though, and made clear that they wanted E.D. placed in a regular classroom without special-education instruction."

"They sought what they referred to as a 'section 504 plan'—after section 504 of the Rehabilitation Act—which would have provided E.D. with some of the educational accommodations otherwise available under the IDEA but without the specialized classes. The negotiations between E.D.'s parents and the school lasted for approximately a year. Twice the school offered an IDEA plan—more commonly known as an Individualized Education Program or 'IEP'—instead of the section 504 plan his parents envisioned. The IEPs would have provided all the iPad-related accommodations his parents sought but would have required him to attend special-education classes. E.D.'s parents rejected both IEPs. The second time, they reiterated their desire for a section 504 plan. Palmyra again refused, and with no resolution in sight, E.D.'s parents pulled him out of school just two weeks after he started first grade."

"In their complaint, E.D.'s parents sought what they had all along: for E.D. to use an iPad to complete his classroom assignments and for his teachers to adapt their teaching methods to incorporate it. They also requested additional accommodations, including a change to the school's testing formats to account for E.D.'s speech and fine motor issues and more time for him to complete his assignments, tests, and homework."

"Palmyra moved for summary judgment on the theory that E.D.'s parents had failed to exhaust the IDEA's administrative procedures. Even though E.D.'s parents had neither sued nor accepted services under the IDEA, Palmyra claimed that they were still required to exhaust their administrative remedies because they were seeking relief that is also available under the IDEA. E.D.'s parents viewed their refusal to accept services as a total opt-out, excusing any failure to comply with the IDEA's procedural requirements. The district court disagreed and granted summary judgment to Palmyra."

"Palmyra moved for summary judgment on the theory that E.D.'s parents had failed to exhaust the

IDEA's administrative procedures. Even though E.D.'s parents had neither sued nor accepted services under the IDEA, Palmyra claimed that they were still required to exhaust their administrative remedies because they were seeking relief that is also available under the IDEA. E.D.'s parents viewed their refusal to accept services as a total opt-out, excusing any failure to comply with the IDEA's procedural requirements. The district court disagreed and granted summary judgment to Palmyra."

"The complaint in this case includes only claims expressly listed in the first half of the statute, so all that is in dispute here is the second half, and specifically whether the relief sought is also available under the IDEA. E.D.'s parents would have us recognize a categorical exception to the exhaustion requirement for parents who refuse all IDEA services. We decline to do so."

"Section 1415(l)'s plain language precludes the exception they seek. All parents, not just those who have previously sought or accepted IDEA services, must exhaust the IDEA's administrative procedures if the relief they seek is also available under the IDEA."

"We have little trouble concluding that the relief E.D.'s parents seek is available under the IDEA. IDEA exhaustion, as the Supreme Court has recently made clear, 'hinges on whether a lawsuit seeks relief for a denial of a free appropriate public education.' *Fry*, 137 S. Ct. at 754. If it does, then exhaustion must occur first. *Id.* If, however, the lawsuit seeks relief 'for simple discrimination,' only tangentially related to education because the discriminatory acts just happened to take place in a school, then exhaustion is unnecessary. *See id.* at 754-56 (explaining that a 'simple discrimination' claim would include 'a wheelchair-bound child who sues his school for discrimination . . . because the building lacks access ramps)."

"It makes no difference that they refused all services under the IDEA. Opting out of IDEA services does not unlock a pathway around exhaustion. Indeed, the statute on which E.D.'s parents most heavily rely, 20 U.S.C. § 1414(a)(1)(D), says only that the school must get the parents' informed consent before providing services under the IDEA, not that a lack of consent will permit them to blow past the exhaustion requirement. *See id.* § 1414(a)(1)(D)(i)(II), (ii)(II). Accordingly, we conclude that Palmyra was entitled to summary judgment."

[**Wrightslaw Note**: That preceding statute is located in our ***Wrightslaw: Special Education Law, 2nd Ed.*** book at pages 93 and 94. It explains that parental consent for an evaluation is not consent for the school to provide services. It further notes that "If the parent of such child refuses to consent to services under clause (i)(II), the local educational agency shall not provide special education and related services to the child by utilizing the procedures described in Section 1415 of this title." In other words, the school cannot initiate a special education due process hearing against the parent for the parent's refusal to consent to services. However, the essence of this case is that if the parent wants the above-desired accommodations under Section 504 but does not want an IEP, the parent must first pursue a special education due process hearing prior to filing a lawsuit in federal or state court.]

The Court of Appeals upheld the ruling of the District Court that the parents failed to exhaust their administrative remedies and thus the case was dismissed in favor of the school district.

Outcome: The school district prevailed.

Return to the Table of Cases

Solorio v. Clovis Unif. Sch. Dist.
9th Circuit
1/15/2019 - California

In this brief, three-paragraph ruling, the Court of Appeals upheld the rulings of the ALJ and District Court Judge finding that the school district provided FAPE in the least restrictive environment. The factual and legal issues are not discussed except that the Ninth Circuit notes that "the ALJ was in the best position to determine the credibility of the relevant witnesses, . . . and he offered sound reasons for finding McVay's testimony to be unpersuasive . . . [and] In balancing the relevant *Rachel H.* factors, the ALJ found that the factors concerning educational and non-academic benefits weighed in favor of a conclusion that the proposed IEP was a FAPE in the LRE, and that those factors outweighed the disruptiveness and cost factor."

Outcome: The school district prevailed.

Return to the Table of Cases

Renee J. v. Houston ISD
5th Circuit
913 F. 3d 523
Judge Jones
1/16/2019 - Texas

In this "transition plan" case, the Fifth Circuit explained that "C.J. is a seventeen-year old male student who has been diagnosed with Autism, intellectual disabilities including an IQ of 51, and Attention Deficit Hyperactivity Disorder (ADHD). He received no formal diagnosis until he was twelve years old and no specialized treatment plan until he was fifteen. He currently reads at a first-grade level. C.J. also has difficulty regulating his emotions and has allegedly been bullied at school."

"C.J.'s Individualized Education Program (IEP) for the 2013-14 school year (his seventh-grade year) revealed that he had not been tested at the district-wide level since third grade and that his math and reading comprehension levels were below those of the average second-grader. When C.J. began eighth grade, however, his district-wide test results from third grade were again carried over to his IEP. C.J.'s transition planning program (a program required for students receiving IEPs under the IDEA) focused on preparing C.J. for a career as a police officer — as it did for several years — even though C.J.'s autism and other learning disabilities render such a career impossible."

"After being homebound for almost a year, C.J. began ninth grade in fall 2015. His attendance was inconsistent and marked by altercations with other students and multiple stints in full-day counseling programs instead of classes . . . his advancement was impeded by his infrequent attendance . . . [A] n independent psychologist . . . recommended that C.J.'s IEP include the use of Applied Behavioral Analysis (ABA), which is one of several therapeutic methods of instruction for children with autism. HISD does not use ABA programs as such, but it does incorporate some ABA methods into its approach."

Parents requested "an administrative due process hearing under the IDEA on December 8, 2015, alleging that HISD failed to provide him a FAPE during his eighth and ninth-grade years. A four-day hearing took place between May 31 and June 6, 2016. The hearing officer considered the testimony of twenty-one witnesses and approximately 2,800 pages of exhibits. Both parties submitted written closing arguments. The hearing officer made credibility determinations to resolve conflicting accounts provided by C.J.'s parents and school personnel. For example, the hearing officer concluded that C.J.'s lack of attendance during the spring of 2015 was caused by his parents' refusal to send him to school, not by HISD's failure to have an appropriate program in place for his education. The hearing officer ultimately concluded that HISD provided C.J. with a FAPE even though its performance had been imperfect."

"C.J.'s parents sought review of the hearing officer's decision in federal district court, but the district court upheld the hearing officer's determinations and granted summary judgment to HISD on all counts. C.J.'s parents timely appealed to this court."

The Fifth Circuit explained that "This court uses a four-factor test established in *Michael F.* to evaluate whether an IEP complies with the IDEA. The factors include whether (1) the student's program is individualized on the basis of the student's assessment and performance; (2) the program is administered in the least restrictive environment; (3) the services are provided in a coordinated and collaborative manner by the key 'stakeholders'; and (4) positive academic and non-academic benefits are demonstrated. This court has never specified precisely how these factors must be weighed.

[**Wrightslaw Note:** *Michael F.* is *Cypress-Fairbanks Indep. Sch. Dist. v. Michael F.*, 118 F.3d 245 (5th Cir. 1997)]

"C.J.'s parents and amici contend that HISD's failure to use ABA programs denied C.J. a FAPE by predetermining his special education recommendations instead of considering his unique needs. Predetermination occurs when the state makes educational decisions too early in the planning process, in a way that deprives the parents of a meaningful opportunity to fully participate as equal members of the IEP team."

With regard to his desire to become a police officer, the Court explained that "Although it is certainly reasonable to believe that C.J.'s disabilities render his prospects of becoming a police officer improbable, autism is a spectrum and so is the set of skills needed for his daily living as well as various jobs. This court is mindful of its obligation not to stray into the field of education policymaking and is reluctant to say, as a matter of law, that HISD was required to communicate a nuanced transition plan in a different way. The evidence reflected that HISD attempted to collaborate with C.J.'s parents in preparing the transition plan. Significantly, C.J.'s later transition plans attempted to engage his principal future employment interest while developing basic life skills necessary for post-secondary life. Thus, we affirm the district court's decision that C.J.'s transition plan did not deny him a FAPE."

The Fifth Circuit upheld the rulings of the Administrative Law Judge and District Court.

Outcome: School prevailed.

Return to the Table of Cases

P.F. v. Taylor, Supt DOE
7th Circuit
Judge Sykes
1/22/2019 - Wisconsin

In this Section 504/ADA disability discrimination case, a group of parents sued Taylor, the Wisconsin State Superintendent of Instruction for the public schools where an "open-enrollment" program distinguished between regular and special education students.

"Under Wisconsin's open-enrollment program, a public-school student can apply to transfer from his resident school district to a nonresident district that has an available space for him. The program distinguishes between 'regular education and special education spaces.' If a student with a disability requires special services, a nonresident district may deny the student's transfer application if it lacks the services or space necessary to meet those special needs."

"This suit concerns a group of disabled schoolchildren whose transfer applications were denied because nonresident districts determined that they could not meet the students' special needs. The students' parents, on their children's behalf, sued the school districts and various state actors seeking injunctive, declaratory, and compensatory relief under Title II of the Americans with Disabilities Act (ADA), 42 U.S.C. § 12132; section 504 of the Rehabilitation Act, 29 U.S.C. § 794(a); and the Equal Protection Clause, U.S. CONST. amend. XIV, § 1. They argued that the program unlawfully discriminates against disabled children because of their disabilities. The district judge concluded that the program did not violate federal law and entered summary judgment for the defendants."

"We affirm. Differential treatment of special-needs students doesn't make the program unlawful. Federal law forbids discrimination based on stereotypes about a handicap, but it does not forbid decisions based on the actual attributes of the handicap. The program makes decisions based on the actual needs of disabled students, so it complies with federal law. And even if we analyze the case as a request for an accommodation, the requested change would fundamentally alter the program, and neither the ADA nor the Rehabilitation Act require fundamental alterations."

"Most applications are accepted, including those submitted by students with IEPs. In 2013-2014, districts approved 3,718 out of 5,822 transfer applications for students with IEPs, or roughly 64%. The same year districts approved 71% of transfer applications for students without IEPs."

"The plaintiffs do not contend that the State Superintendent, the Department, or any of the school districts intentionally deviated from the program in a discriminatory manner. Rather, they claim that the program itself discriminates on the basis of disability and that the defendants are liable for their role in administering it. The question before us, then, is whether the open-enrollment program, by its terms, violates federal antidiscrimination law."

"It does not. The plaintiffs argue that the program discriminates against disabled students because it imposes criteria that apply only to students with special needs. But their argument rests on mischaracterizations of federal law and the program itself. Under federal law a program is not discriminatory just because it takes an individual's disability into account. Although a disability is not a permissible ground for assuming an inability to function in a particular context, the disability is not thrown out when considering if the person is qualified. Put another way, federal law forbids discrimination based on stereotypes about a handicap, but it does not forbid decisions based on the actual attributes of the handicap."

"Under the open-enrollment program, nonresident districts cannot turn away applicants merely because they are disabled. Instead the program allows nonresident districts to realistically assess whether they have the capacity and resources to comply with a transfer student's IEP. Because decisions are based on a student's special needs, the program hinges on the actual attributes of the handicap rather than mere stereotypes."

Outcome: The state prevailed, a nonresident school district may deny a special education student's transfer application because of the child's disability.

Return to the Table of Cases

M.S. v. Los Angeles Unif. Sch. Dist.
9th Circuit
913 F. 3d 1119
1/24/2019 - California

This case concerns residential placement for mental health vis á vis educational purposes.

When M.S. was four years old, she "witnessed her mother's death." Her father was absent and she lived with her grandparents for several years and then was removed from them because of neglect and "abuse and caretaker incapacity." She was in the care of the Los Angeles County Department of Children and Family Services (DCFS) since she was eleven years old with numerous foster home, residential care, and mental health hospital placements and was a ward of the juvenile court.

At the time of the due process hearing initiated by her "educational rights holder" she had been released from "juvenile hall" and was placed in the locked residential treatment facility known as "The Vista."

The short, five-paragraph Ninth Circuit ruling does not provide the factual or legal history. It incorporates by reference and refers the reader to "Appendix A" of its decision which was the District Court's detailed history and ruling. The preceding facts were taken from that District Court opinion.

At issue is the school's appeal of the District Court which reversed the ruling of the Administrative Law Judge. The Ninth Circuit explained that "The district court correctly concluded that M.S. was denied a FAPE because LAUSD was required to consider whether a residential placement should be offered to M.S. for educational purposes as part of her individualized education plan (IEP) notwithstanding that another county agency, the Department of Children and Family Services (DCFS), had residentially placed her for mental health treatment under state law, and pursuant to a Juvenile Court order. In a thorough and well-reasoned opinion, the district court concluded that the LAUSD had an independent obligation to ensure that a continuum of alternative placements was available to meet M.S.'s educational needs and to consider whether a residential placement was necessary for educational purposes and not merely necessary quite apart from the learning process."

The Court of Appeals concluded with the statement that "We agree with the district court's conclusion, and affirm for the reasons stated in the district court's Memorandum and Decision, reissued January 9, 2019, and attached hereto as Appendix A."

[**Wrightslaw Note**: Appendix A was not included in the Google case, but is available at: http://cdn.ca9.uscourts.gov/datastore/opinions/2019/01/24/16-56472.pdf]

Outcome: The child prevailed and case remanded to the ALJ to determine appropriate relief for denial of FAPE.

Return to the Table of Cases

Colonial School District v. G.K.
3rd Circuit
Judge Porter
2/13/2019 - Pennsylvania

This is an IEP lack of progress/immeasurable goals case. Parents prevailed at due process and the school appealed to the U.S. District Court, which reversed.

On appeal, the Third Circuit explained that "G.K. is a student at Colonial who requires special education due to autism and learning disabilities in reading comprehension, written expression, math problem-solving, and social language and social skills. Following G.K.'s fourth grade year (2015-16), Parents requested that he be held back rather than advance to fifth grade. Colonial denied this request, stating that G.K. showed excellent improvement academically and socially and that it would not be appropriate or beneficial for him to be older than his fourth grade classmates."

"Colonial and Parents could not agree on the appropriate grade for G.K., so Parents filed a due process complaint. The parties entered into mediation, and Parents eventually agreed that G.K. would advance to fifth grade. In exchange, Colonial agreed to (1) hold an IEP meeting in September 2016 to discuss G.K.'s learning goals, (2) provide Parents with standardized testing scores, and (3) pay for an Independent Educational Evaluation for G.K."

"Parents and Colonial met in September 2016 to discuss G.K.'s learning goals. At Parents' request, Colonial agreed to create objectives to address G.K.'s deficient areas. Colonial also agreed to assign daily homework based on the IEP, provide Parents with specific progress notes, and meet again in November 2016 to discuss G.K.'s progress."

"After the September 2016 meeting, even though Colonial updated the IEP to reflect Parents' input, Parents filed a second due process complaint. Though the updated IEP added new annual goals, Parents thought it still failed to address the deficiencies identified in the end-of-school-year assessments. They requested that Colonial pay for a third party to develop new IEP goals."

"After three hearing sessions in 2017 to evaluate the reasonableness of the September 2016 IEP, a hearing officer ruled for Parents, and Colonial appealed. The District Court reversed, concluding that the hearing officer improperly considered whether G.K. made sufficient progress under the IEP, exaggerated the importance of minor shortcomings in the IEP, and erroneously characterized Parents' alleged lack of subjective understanding as a denial of parent participation. Parents timely appealed."

The Third Circuit explained that "The hearing officer relied on post-IEP performance to evaluate the IEP. Not only did the hearing officer expressly include G.K.'s progress in his statement of the issues, he also based his decision on his finding that G.K. did not make progress . . . on certain goals in the IEP . . . the District Court reasonably rejected the hearing officer's undue reliance on G.K.'s post-IEP performance."

"The District Court correctly overturned the

hearing officer's finding that G.K.'s IEP was fatally flawed under the IDEA. Parents' claim that the IEP's goals were immeasurable was not a substantive error nor a procedural error that violated G.K.'s right to a free appropriate public education. The District Court also rightly concluded that Parents' dissatisfaction with the IEP was not a denial of meaningful participation under IDEA. For these reasons, we will affirm the District Court's judgment."

Outcome: The school district prevailed.

Return to the Table of Cases

Ricks v. Hawaii State Dept. of Ed.
9th Circuit
2/13/2019 - Hawaii

In this case, which went to a jury, the parent's lawsuit alleged that the use of a Rifton Chair violated Section 504 and, by using the chair, school staff were guilty of assault and battery and inflicted emotional distress upon their child. In Hawaii, the local school district and the State Department of Education are the same. The state is both the LEA and the SEA.

Prior to the jury trial, the District Court judge dismissed the assault, battery, and intentional infliction of distress claims finding that there was no malice and that the defendants had a qualified immunity. The Section 504 allegation was heard by a jury and, after four days, the verdict was in favor of Hawaii. The parents appealed "the district court's rulings on evidence and the jury instructions" to the Ninth Circuit.

The Ninth Circuit explained that "The undisputed fact that use of the Rifton chair was not documented in M.R.'s Individualized Education Program (IEP) or Behavioral Plan, standing alone, is insufficient to render the DOE liable as a matter of law under Section 504 for violating 34 C.F.R. § 104.33(b). Implementing an IEP developed in accordance with the Individuals with Disabilities Education Act is only one means of ensuring compliance with 34 C.F.R. § 104.33(b)(1)(i)'s requirement that educational aids and services are 'designed to meet individual educational needs.' Therefore, it does not follow that the use of a Rifton chair, above and beyond the aids and services listed in the IEP, necessarily violates Section 504's regulations requiring provision of a free and appropriate public education (FAPE)."

"We conclude the district court did not err in formulating the final instructions to the jury. The court drew a careful distinction between a claim for denial of a FAPE under the IDEA, which could not be adjudicated in this case because it was unexhausted, and a claim of discrimination based on the denial of meaningful access to public education under Section 504."

[**Wrightslaw Note:** For another case where a child was restrained in a desk/chair, see the 2015 *Ebonie S. v. Pueblo School District* case in which a Jury awarded $2.2M. Link to the Complaint is here and the link to the Jury Instructions is here and the link to the Jury Verdict is here.]

Outcome: The Hawaii DOE prevailed.

Return to the Table of Cases

Ms. S. v. Regional School Unit 72
1st Circuit
916 F. 3d 41
Judge Lynch
2/15/2019 - Maine

"These appeals stem from a complaint filed by Ms. S. with the Maine Department of Education (MDOE) in May 2013 alleging violations of the Individuals with Disabilities Education Act (IDEA). The state due process hearing officer dismissed as untimely Ms. S.'s claims about her son B.S.'s education in school years 2009-2010 and 2010-2011 and found no violations as to school years 2011-2012 and 2012-2013."

Maine's Unified Special Education Regulation (MUSER) previously provided a four-year statute of limitations. Later it was revised to two years.

It was alleged that the revision process did not comply with Maine's administrative rules in regard to regulatory revisions and thus should remain at four years. The District Court judge agreed and, on remand, re-opened the case to include a determination as to the 2009-2010 and 2010-2011 school years. This case was previously before the First Circuit on July 15, 2016, and is in our 2016 Year in Review book. [URL is https://www.wrightslaw.com/store/2016law.html]

"In this second decision from this court, we hold that Maine has established a two-year statute of limitations for due process complaints and that it has done so to align its statute of limitations with the IDEA's. Ms. S.'s claims about 2009-2010 and 2010-2011 are thus time barred. More specifically, we reverse the district court's ruling . . . that Ms. S.'s claims were timely."

"We hold that Maine intended to adopt a two-year limitations period that mirrors the IDEA's timing provisions. This intent is evident from the language of the provisions: as noted, MUSER § XVI.5.A(2) mirrors 20 U.S.C. § 1415(b)(6)(B) and MUSER § XVI.13.E mirrors 20 U.S.C. § 1414(f)(C)(3)."

"So, we turn to the IDEA to determine how to read MUSER. The federal Department of Education stated in 2016 that 'the statute of limitations in section 1415(b)(6)(B) is the same as the statute of limitations in section 1415(f)(3)(C).' We hold that the IDEA has a single two-year statute of limitations regulating the amount of time to file a complaint after the reasonable discovery date. In holding this, we join the Third and Ninth Circuits."

"We remand with instructions to dismiss her action with prejudice."

However, the dissenting Judge asserted that "If the MDOE wants to change the governing four-year statute of limitations, it must do so the right way. Unlike my colleagues, I cannot condone the MDOE's improper adoption of the reduced filing deadline, contrary to the public disclosures required by law, or the resulting unfair refusal to consider Ms. S.'s claims concerning her son's ninth and tenth grade years. I therefore respectfully dissent."

Outcome: The school district prevailed.

Return to the Table of Cases

Barney v. Akron Bd. Ed.
6th Circuit
Judge Kethledge
2/25/2019 - Ohio

The Sixth Circuit explained that "Delaina Barney argues that the Akron Board of Education violated the Individuals with Disabilities Education Act in nearly a dozen ways. The district court rejected all her arguments. We affirm." In a separate proceeding, discussed at the end of this case, attorney's fees were assessed against Barney's attorneys.

The parent lost at due process, at the state review level, before the U.S. District Court and again before the Court of Appeals. That Court noted that "Delaina Barney's son, J.B., has cognitive disabilities and a peanut allergy. J.B. has received special education for his cognitive disabilities since preschool. J.B. has not received special services under the Act for his allergy, but his school had a medical plan for preventing and responding to allergic reactions. Among other safeguards, the school had instructed food servers not to bring peanut butter to J.B.'s classroom when serving students their free breakfast."

The parent asserted "that J.B.'s program should have addressed his peanut allergy. Yet the district noted that J.B. had a peanut allergy in his written individualized-education program under the heading, 'other information.' And the school district had a separate medical plan to address his allergy. The Act does not require more."

While in the third grade, "Barney met with J.B.'s teachers to discuss his individualized education program. The teachers described J.B.'s academic progress, as well as his behavioral improvements since he began taking Ritalin for his ADHD. Barney was moved to tears when she heard about J.B.'s progress, and signed off on the proposed program without objection. Two days later, however, Barney removed J.B. from the school."

"Barney thereafter filed a complaint with the Ohio Department of Education under the Act, challenging the school district's response to J.B.'s peanut allergy and the district's implementation of J.B.'s educational program. After a hearing, the Department of Education ruled for the school district. Barney appealed the decision to a state-level review officer, who affirmed. Barney then brought this lawsuit. The district court likewise entered judgment in favor of the district. Barney now appeals."

Among the numerous allegations, she argued "that the district violated the Act by failing to consider whether J.B. would benefit from an extended school year. But the record shows that Barney attended a meeting where school officials did discuss an extended school year, and that she said nothing when they decided that J.B. was not eligible for those services. Hence Barney has not shown that the district violated the Act on this ground."

"Barney next argues that the school district violated the Act by failing to provide copies of J.B.'s educational records, which in turn prevented her from obtaining an independent expert's opinion about the adequacy of J.B.'s program. But the record belies this argument. During the administrative proceedings, Barney conceded that she had received these records prior to the first hearing."

Barney "takes issue with J.B.'s program, which she says was not sufficiently ambitious or specific. Contrary to Barney's assertion, however, the program contained goals tailored to J.B.'s weaknesses in five categories: speech, fine motor skills, reading, writing, and math. Each goal included detailed academic objectives. Moreover, the program specified how much time should be spent weekly on each goal and provided for regular reporting of J.B.'s progress to his parents. Barney therefore has not shown why the program was not reasonably calculated to enable J.B. to make progress appropriate in light of his circumstances."

"Barney argues that the school district violated the Act's mandate to educate J.B. in the 'least restrictive environment'—that is, to educate J.B. alongside non-disabled children to the maximum extent appropriate. In support of that argument, Barney asserts that she had to drive J.B. to a field trip, which isolated J.B. from his classmates who traveled on a school bus. But Barney herself insisted on driving J.B. out of fear that he might be exposed to peanut butter on the bus. She cannot blame the school district for her own decision to separate J.B. from his peers."

"Barney next argues that J.B.'s program was not reasonably calculated to address his unique problems. Specifically, she says that J.B. was bullied at school and that the district should have addressed the bullying in his educational program. But Barney never told the school about the bullying—even when she was explicitly asked about bullying in a questionnaire for J.B.'s reevaluation. And Barney does not explain why the district should have otherwise identified bullying as a problem that was severe enough to warrant modification to J.B.'s educational program."

"Finally, Barney contends that the school district should have addressed problems resulting from J.B.'s transfers among various schools in the district (all of which transfers Barney initiated). But Barney nowhere explains what the district should have done differently because of those transfers. She therefore has not shown that J.B's educational program was not 'reasonably calculated' to enable J.B. to make 'progress appropriate in light of his circumstances.'"

[**Wrightslaw Note**: The parent filed numerous allegations against the school district. Not all are included above. Her appeal to the District Court included new allegations and legal theories which were summarily dismissed.]

In another related case, the school district sought attorney's fees against the parents attorney. The District Court found that the "due process complaint was frivolous, unreasonable, and without foundation when filed . . . [and that her attorneys] initiated the due process complaint and continued to litigate its claims even after it had become patently obvious that their claims were meritless . . ." [Google Scholar link here.]

[**Wrightslaw Note:** On March 13, 2019 one of her attorneys filed bankruptcy and submitted the proof of such filing with the District Court.]

Outcome: The school district prevailed.

Return to the Table of Cases

Oliver C. v. Hawaii DOE
9th Circuit
3/5/2019 - Hawaii

This case is the Ninth Circuit's interpretation of the "stay-put" statute, also known in other parts of the country as the "pendency statute." In Hawaii, the local education agency (LEA) is also the State Education Agency (SEA). Hawaii classifies portions of the state as school districts; however, they are not known as separate school districts and separate LEA's as is customary in the continental USA (CONUS).

With regard to the facts, the Court explained that "Oliver C. is a preschool student who qualifies for special education services. In September 2016, Oliver's family moved from the Honolulu District to the Windward School District across the island. The Windward Department of Education (DOE) determined that Benjamin Parker Elementary in the Windward District could implement Oliver's Individualized Education Program (IEP). In October 2016, Oliver's parents objected to this determination and filed a request for mediation and a due process hearing, and they sought a stay-put order from the Office of Administrative Hearings for the Department of Commerce and Consumer Affairs to allow Oliver to remain at his school in Honolulu during all proceedings. On February 22, 2017, a Hearing Officer denied Oliver's parents' stay-put request and held that Benjamin Parker was the appropriate placement for the 2016-2017 school year. The district court affirmed."

"On appeal, Oliver's parents argue that the Hearing Officer erred by denying the stay-put order under § 1415(j) of the Individuals with Disabilities Education Act (IDEA) because moving Oliver from Kuhio to Benjamin Parker would significantly change his educational placement."

"The IDEA's stay-put provision states that 'during the pendency of any proceedings conducted [under the IDEA] . . . [a] child shall remain in [his] then-current educational placement.' 20 U.S.C. § 1415(j). [*See* ***Wrightslaw: Special Education Law, 2nd Ed.***, page 118.] We define 'current educational placement' as the placement set forth in the child's last implemented IEP. A change in location alone does not qualify as a change in 'educational placement.' Rather, a change in placement occurs when there is a significant change in the student's program. A change in location alone would not substantially or materially alter the child's educational program."

The Court of Appeals upheld the Hearing Officer and District Court's finding that the physical move was not a change of placement triggering the stay-put statute.

Outcome: The school district prevailed.

Return to the Table of Cases

R.F. v. Cecil County Public Schools
4th Circuit
919 F. 3d 237
Judge Duncan
3/25/2019 - Maryland

Parents lost at Due Process, District Court, and before the Fourth Circuit which noted that parents alleged that "CCPS violated the IDEA by (1) failing to educate R.F. in the least restrictive environment, (2) failing to implement R.F.'s Individualized Education Program, (3) denying R.F.'s parents the opportunity to participate in her educational decisionmaking, and (4) providing an IEP that was inappropriate for R.F.'s needs. The ALJ found, and the district court agreed, that while CCPS violated certain procedural requirements of the IDEA, those violations did not substantively deny R.F. a

FAPE in violation of the IDEA."

The primary issue of this case concerns whether a procedural violation can result in denial of FAPE, thus opening the door to a private school special education placement.

The Fourth Circuit explained that "R.F. has been diagnosed with severe autism spectrum disorder and a rare genetic disorder. She generally communicates without using words, and she exhibits complex, challenging, disruptive behaviors such as hyperactivity and aggression. Her aggressive behaviors, which include grabbing people, pulling hair, biting, and placing her mouth on others, often manifest during transitions in the school day. R.F. also exhibits physical limitations—for instance, she has significant neuromuscular deficits, so she sometimes needs assistance sitting up straight and being aware of her body's position when navigating steps and curbs. R.F. requires adult supervision and assistance at all times. She also has a short attention span and has difficulty processing information quickly."

"R.F.'s IEP team—comprised primarily of CCPS staff and R.F.'s parents—met in May 2016 to revise her IEP for the 2016-2017 first grade school year (the May 2016 IEP). The May 2016 IEP incorporated R.F.'s BIP. It also included thirteen goals to address R.F.'s academic, behavioral, physical, and speech and language needs. The IEP team determined that to make progress on these goals, R.F. would require sixteen hours and fifty-five minutes outside the general education setting and fourteen hours and thirty-five minutes inside the general education setting each week."

"R.F.'s mother attended this meeting and objected to the May 2016 IEP. She did not think that R.F. should be included in classes with nondisabled peers and requested that CCPS pay for R.F.'s tuition at the Benedictine School, a private school. The other members of R.F.'s IEP team disagreed and noted that CCPS was developing an intensive communication support classroom (an ICSC) for children with communicative difficulties. The IEP team again met in June 2016 to evaluate R.F.'s progress on her IEP goals before the start of the 2016-2017 school year. Appellants' arguments on appeal focus solely on the 2016-2017 school year."

"At the start of the 2016-2017 school year, CCPS provided most of R.F.'s special education services in the ICSC. Although CCPS anticipated the participation of other students in the ICSC, those students did not attend in the fall of 2016 due to unexpected circumstances. Consequently, R.F. was the only student in the ICSC. R.F. joined the general education classroom for 'specials' (e.g. gym, art, music), recess, field trips, and occasional reading and math classes."

"Mr. K., a special education teacher, provided R.F. with special education services in the ICSC. CCPS also assigned a paraprofessional to support R.F. throughout the day. In the ICSC and throughout R.F.'s day, CCPS offered R.F. a number of specialized services, including individualized supervision and instruction, and supports. These supports included objects meant to help R.F. transition to new activities and locations, a visual schedule with verbal cues, and low lighting and reduced noise."

"CCPS implemented the BIP regularly, but not perfectly. For instance, while Mr. K. used the behavior reduction and intervention steps in the BIP, he did not always follow them in order. To monitor R.F.'s progress toward her IEP goals, Mr. K. collected data on R.F.'s behavior and performance every other week and incorporated that data into quarterly progress reports. He destroyed his raw data after writing the quarterly reports, even though CCPS requires teachers to maintain data for two years."

"In August 2016, approximately three weeks after the start of school, Mr. K. began to notice that R.F. struggled when she joined her nondisabled peers in the general education setting. She had difficulty walking between classrooms and staying seated and quiet in the general education classroom. She also often failed to finish her lunch in the school lunchroom because she became distracted."

"In response to these difficulties, Mr. K. gradually began providing more instruction to R.F. in the ICSC instead of the general education classroom.

For instance, while R.F.'s schedule placed her in the general education classroom for reading comprehension, Mr. K. would sometimes remove her from that class and take her back to the ICSC. This decision varied daily and, according to Mr. K., was 'responsive to her needs depending on her success in the class.' On some days, Mr. K. was unable to take R.F. to the general education classroom 'if she was exhibiting really aggressive behaviors or if she was having a really difficult time walking or with mobility.' As a result of these adjustments, R.F.'s hours in the ICSC exceeded the number specified in the May 2016 IEP."

"In December 2016, R.F.'s IEP team met again to revise her IEP (the 'December 2016 IEP). The team decided to reduce the number of hours that R.F. spent in the general education setting so that she would only attend specials with nondisabled peers. Accordingly, the December 2016 IEP increased R.F.'s weekly time outside the general education setting from sixteen hours and fifty-five minutes to twenty-nine hours."

"R.F.'s parents attended the meeting and opposed CCPS's approach. R.F.'s mother again expressed opposition to placing R.F. in a general education setting 'at all during the school day.' R.F.'s parents also presented a report by Lisa Frank, an education consultant, who recommended placement in a 'full-day evidence-based program for children with autism' like the Benedictine School. *Id.* The other members of the IEP team disagreed with this proposed placement and determined that the ICSC was the best placement for R.F."

"Shortly after R.F.'s IEP team compiled the December 2016 IEP, R.F.'s parents initiated this action, alleging that CCPS violated the IDEA and seeking to have R.F. placed at the Benedictine School or another private school at CCPS's expense."

"As relevant to one of Appellants' principal claims concerning CCPS's procedural violations of the statute, Mr. K. stated that he was unaware that CCPS required teachers to maintain raw data for two years. The ALJ concluded that he had violated CCPS's retention policy but 'did not do so for any nefarious purpose,' and she declined to draw any negative inferences from his testimony."

"Based on the testimony and data presented at the hearing, the ALJ evaluated R.F.'s progress on her IEP goals. She found that R.F. had made progress toward some of her physical goals as well as some of her speech and language goals. She also found that R.F. did not make progress toward her behavioral or academic goals. She concluded that, overall, R.F. had 'made incremental progress on some, but not all of her goals' and that this was appropriate for R.F. 'given her unique circumstances.' "

"The ALJ issued a decision holding that CCPS procedurally violated the IDEA by changing R.F.'s placement in August 2016 by gradually increasing her hours in the ICSC without notifying her parents or revising her IEP. She also concluded, however, that this violation did not deny R.F. a FAPE, crediting Mr. K.'s testimony that R.F. was having difficulty in the general education setting and benefited from additional time in the ICSC. Overall, the ALJ concluded that CCPS offered R.F. an IEP reasonably calculated to enable her to make progress appropriate in light of the child's circumstances."

"Under § 1415(f)(3)(E)(ii)(II), an ALJ must answer each of the following in the affirmative to find that a procedural violation of the parental rights provisions of the IDEA constitutes a violation of the IDEA: (1) whether the plaintiffs alleg[ed] a procedural violation, (2) whether that violation significantly impeded the parents' opportunity to participate in the decisionmaking process regarding the provision of a [FAPE] to the parents' child, and (3) whether the child did not receive a [FAPE] as a result. *Id.* § 1415(f)(3)(E). Unless an ALJ determines that a given procedural violation denied the child a FAPE, she may only order compliance with the IDEA's procedural requirements and cannot grant other forms of relief, such as private placement or compensatory education."

"Our analysis here starts and ends with the second prong of this standard: whether a violation of parents' procedural rights under the IDEA significantly impeded their opportunity to participate in decisionmaking regarding their child's education. Appellants contend that CCPS violated their parental participation rights under the IDEA by changing R.F.'s placement without involving them in an IEP meeting and by destroying data relating to R.F.'s progress on her IEP goals. We hold that neither constitutes a significant impediment to parental participation on these facts."

"The IEP did not aim for grade-level advancement through the general curriculum or for standard letter grades because these were not considered a reasonable prospect for R.F. But this does not indicate a failure to set challenging objectives for R.F. The IEP team also revised the IEP in December 2016 to account for the progress that R.F. had made to date."

"This combination of reasonably ambitious goals that were focused on R.F.'s particular circumstances and that were pursued through the careful and attentive instruction of specialized professionals provided the education that R.F. is entitled to under the statute. We therefore conclude that CCPS provided R.F. with a FAPE despite its procedural violations of the IDEA."

"Although CCPS procedurally violated the IDEA in certain technical respects, it did not substantively violate the IDEA because it did not deny R.F. a FAPE. We therefore AFFIRM."

[**Wrightslaw Note:** A Petition for Certiorari was filed with the U.S. Supreme Court, which was denied.]

Outcome: The school district prevailed.

Return to the Table of Cases

E.M. v. Lewisville Indep. Sch. Dist.
5th Circuit
4/1/2019 - Texas

In this short, three-paragraph opinion, the Fifth Circuit upheld the rulings by the ALJ and District Court in this speech impairment case.

The Court explained that "E.M., a third-grade student with autism, a speech impairment, orthopedic impairment, cerebral palsy, intellectual disability, and childhood apraxia of speech, [filed suit contending that] . . . E.M. would not have received a free appropriate public education under the challenged 2013 IEP because it discontinued the assistance of a sign language interpreter and would no longer include as an educational goal improving E.M.'s ability to articulate new letter sounds to form words."

"A special education hearing officer heard testimony from multiple communication and education professionals who worked with and observed E.M. and concluded that LISD had offered her a free appropriate public education in compliance with the IDEA."

On appeal, the District Court "affirmed the hearing officer. Appellants now appeal in this court."

"Our careful review of the record, the parties' briefs, and the district court's opinion demonstrates no error in the decision below. In a detailed opinion, the district court concluded that E.M. had not and was unlikely to make meaningful progress in articulating sounds, did not use her sign language interpreter, and instead communicated primarily and relatively successfully through assistive technology. Applying this court's four-factor test from *Michael F.* to these facts, the district then determined that the challenged IEP was reasonably calculated to enable E.M. to receive educational benefits as required under the IDEA. Finding no error, we AFFIRM the district court's judgment for essentially the same reasons stated by that court."

Outcome: The school district prevailed.

Return to the Table of Cases

Lucas v. Henrico County Sch. Bd.
4th Circuit
4/12/2019 - Virginia

This unusual case involved a parent and two lay advocates filing suit against the school district, school district staff, the police, the state court criminal prosecutor and the state court general district court judge. The parent and advocates were arrested for trespassing at the public school, convicted, and filed suit in federal court.

"In these consolidated cases, Toni Hunter-Davis (Davis), Kandise Lucas, and Dr. Marla Crawford appeal the district court's dismissal with prejudice of their civil complaint against the Henrico County Public School Board (Board), Superintendent Patrick Kinlaw, Principal Kirk Eggleston, the Henrico County Police Department (HCPD), Henrico County Police Chief Humberto Cardounel, Sergeant Crook, Henrico County Commonwealth's Attorney Shannon Taylor, Assistant Commonwealth's Attorney Tania Kregar, and Henrico County District Court Judge L. Neil Steverson."

"Plaintiffs alleged violations of the Individuals with Disabilities Education Act, the Americans with Disabilities Act, the Rehabilitation Act of 1973 and 42 U.S.C. § 1983, along with related state law claims. We affirm in part, vacate in part, and remand for further proceedings."

Plaintiffs' claims arose out of their arrests and criminal prosecutions for trespassing, in violation of Va. Code Ann. 18.2-128, at Colonial Trails Elementary School in Henrico County, Virginia, on January 31, 2018. Plaintiffs were protesting and seeking reversal of the school's decision to involuntarily withdraw Davis' son, M.A., from enrollment, which they alleged violated the IDEA, the ADA, the Rehabilitation Act, and the Equal Protection Clause. They also alleged that Kinlaw, Eggleston, and the Board retaliated against Plaintiffs for attempting to protect M.A.'s rights under the ADA and the Rehabilitation Act. Further, Plaintiffs claimed that their arrests for trespass violated their First and Fourth Amendment rights, and that the prosecutors—Taylor and Kregar—and the judge—Steverson—in their criminal case violated their Fifth, Sixth, Eighth, and Fourteenth Amendment rights." [In a footnote, the Fourth Circuit noted that "Davis entered a plea of no contest, while Lucas and Crawford were convicted at a joint trial."]

The district court dismissed Plaintiffs' IDEA, ADA, Rehabilitation Act, Fourteenth Amendment equal protection and the remaining civil rights claims, either "for lack of standing . . . for failure to state a claim. . . for lack of subject matter jurisdiction . . . [and] declined to exercise supplemental jurisdiction over Plaintiffs' state law claims." Several of the "federal civil rights claims were dismissed for lack of subject matter jurisdiction under the *Rooker-Feldman* doctrine and, alternatively, under the doctrine of *Younger* abstention."

[**Wrightslaw Note**: These are U.S. Supreme Court cases explaining that federal courts should abstain from involvement in ongoing state court proceedings.]

Since the state court criminal proceedings were on appeal, the Fourth Circuit explained that "abstention" should not have resulted in dismissal of the other civil rights claims, but instead that "even if abstention was proper, the district court should have stayed, rather than dismissed, the civil rights claims where, as here, Plaintiffs sought damages as well as declaratory and injunctive relief."

"We conclude, however, that the district court erred in dismissing Plaintiffs' remaining federal civil rights claims under *Rooker-Feldman* and *Younger*."

"Accordingly, we affirm the district court's dismissal of Plaintiffs' IDEA, ADA, and Rehabilitation Act claims and Plaintiffs' equal protection claim. We also affirm the dismissal of Plaintiffs' federal civil rights claims against Taylor, Kregar, and Steverson. We vacate the dismissal of the remaining civil rights claims against the other defendants. Finally, because the district court's decision to decline supplemental jurisdiction over the state law claims was based on its dismissal of all the federal claims, we also vacate that portion of the judgment. We remand these cases to the district court for proceedings consistent with this opinion."

Outcome: The school district and other defendants essentially prevailed. Pending resolution of the state court criminal proceedings, the District Court should have stayed and not dismissed the other claims.

[**Wrightslaw Note:** As a result of this case and a slew of others filed by the same advocate, the Virginia General Assembly created a commission to study regulation of the conduct of lay advocates.]

Return to the Table of Cases

Morales v. Newport-Mesa Unif. Sch. Dist.
9th Circuit
4/24/2019 - California

After Morales graduated from high school, her mother requested a due process hearing against the school district. Halfway through her senior year, Morales "was hit by a car, resulting in life-threatening injuries and traumatic brain injury."

"The Administrative Law Judge (ALJ) concluded that Newport-Mesa failed in its child find duties because, despite having notice about the traumatic brain injury, Newport-Mesa failed to offer Morales's mother an assessment plan to determine Morales's eligibility for special education. The ALJ therefore concluded that Newport-Mesa denied Morales a free appropriate public education (FAPE). The ALJ also concluded that there were no other procedural violations that denied Morales a FAPE and that, for the purposes of the IDEA, Morales graduated with a valid high school diploma. On the basis of the child find violation, the ALJ awarded 40 hours of tutoring (valued at $2,600), a vocational assessment, and an assistive technology assessment."

"Morales timely filed a complaint with the district court, challenging OAH's rulings against her and bringing a claim under Section 504 of the Rehabilitation Act, 29 U.S.C. § 794. The district court affirmed the OAH decision in full and granted Newport-Mesa's motion for summary judgment on the Section 504 claim."

"The record supports the ALJ's determination that Morales's mother received the procedural safeguards required under 34 C.F.R. § 300.504, and that any other procedural violations of Morales's rights were harmless for the reasons identified by the ALJ. A procedural violation does not constitute a denial of a FAPE if the violation fails to result in a loss of educational opportunity."

"Given Morales's generalized request for academic services, transition services, related services, and mental health services, the ALJ did not abuse her discretion in relying on Dr. Nancy Merkel's recommendation of the Fusion Learning Academy. On appeal, Morales failed to articulate the exact services she was requesting, and, Morales's graduation weighs heavily against expanding the remedy already awarded."

"Lastly, the district court did not err in granting summary judgment on Morales's Section 504 claims. Morales has not shown how Newport-Mesa's alleged failure to accommodate her was the result of intentional discrimination or deliberate indifference. Specifically, Morales has not shown a triable issue of fact as to whether Newport-Mesa waived graduation requirements or failed to provide a Section 504 assessment solely on the basis of her disability."

"Under the circumstances presented in this record, we affirm the district court's judgment in all respects."

Outcome: The school district prevailed.

Return to the Table of Cases

R.M. v. Gilbert Unif. Sch. Dist.
9th Circuit
4/29/2019 - California

In this short, three-paragraph decision, the Ninth Circuit upheld the District Court's ruling that the child was provided FAPE in the least restrictive environment.

"Plaintiff argues that the District inappropriately increased his special education service minutes by 20 minutes per day, reducing the time that he spends in the general education classroom. Using the analysis set forth in *Sacramento City Unified School District v. Rachel H.*, 14 F.3d 1398 (9th Cir. 1994), we hold that the school district appropriately increased Plaintiff's special education service minutes by 20 minutes per day . . . [E]ven when the other factors weigh in favor of mainstreaming, the student's academic needs weigh most heavily against a mainstream environment . . . IDEA demands more than de minimis progress. It requires an educational program reasonably calculated to enable a child to make progress appropriate in light of the child's circumstances."

"Additionally, Plaintiff argues that the District's proposed move from Ashland Ranch Elementary to Pioneer Elementary was a change in 'placement' [per *Rachel H.*] . . . First, we hold that this proposal was a change in 'location' only . . . Second, the great weight of the testimony offered during the hearing established that Plaintiff's needs could best be met at Pioneer Elementary because of its Academic SCILLS classroom. Accordingly, the proposed change in location did not violate Plaintiff's rights under the IDEA."

Outcome: The school district prevailed.

Return to the Table of Cases

J.B. v. Hawaii DOE
9th Circuit
5/9/2019 - Hawaii

This case concerns LRE and methodology and "J.B.'s transition from Pacific Autism Center (PAC), a small private school for students with autism and other special needs, into a Hawaii public school named Koko Head Elementary School (Koko Head). During that time, Hawaii Department of Education (DOE) personnel convened to develop an Individualized Education Plan (IEP) for J.B.'s transition. J.B.'s father, R.E.B., raised various objections to J.B.'s proposed IEP, but the administrative hearings officer found that his IEP was adequate. The district court affirmed. R.E.B. then appealed to this court."

The Ninth Circuit explained that "R.E.B. first argues that DOE violated the IDEA by failing to address his concerns about J.B.'s transition from PAC to Koko Head. Particularly, R.E.B. complains that J.B.'s IEP did not specify where J.B.'s summer 2012 Extended School Year (ESY) services would take place when J.B. was transitioning from PAC to Koko Head."

"DOE sufficiently addressed R.E.B.'s concerns about J.B.'s transition services. Although J.B.'s IEP did not specify where J.B.'s summer 2012 ESY services would take place, his IEP listed his current school as Koko Head. Additionally, the IDEA does not require that an IEP list the specific school where summer transition services will take place."

"R.E.B. also contends that DOE violated the IDEA because J.B.'s IEP did not specify the Least Restrictive Environment (LRE) for J.B. J.B.'s IEP states that J.B. will not participate with non-disabled peers for Reading, Writing, Math, Science, Social Studies, Speech/Language Therapy and Occupational Therapy. J.B. will participate with non-disabled peers for Library, Music, PE, Art, Computer, Hawaiian Studies, Mandarin, recesses, lunch, field trips, assemblies and school-wide activities. J.B. will also receive specialized instruction in the general education setting for Science and Social Studies activities as deemed appropriate by his Special Education teacher/Care Coordinator and General Education teacher."

"This explanation sufficiently specifies the LRE for J.B. under the IDEA because J.B.'s IEP team, which included J.B.'s public school principal, future teachers, and R.E.B., decided for all academic subjects, as a general matter, whether J.B. would participate with nondisabled peers. The IEP then delegated to J.B.'s teachers the decision to have J.B. participate with nondisabled peers for certain Science and Social Studies activities even though, as a general matter, J.B. would not participate with nondisabled peers for these subjects."

"Finally, R.E.B. contends that DOE violated the IDEA by not specifying the use of Applied Behavioral Analysis (ABA) methodology in J.B.'s IEP. At PAC, J.B.'s teachers used ABA, a teaching methodology for students with autism. R.E.B. wanted

DOE to specify in J.B.'s IEP that ABA methodology would be used with J.B. At an IEP meeting on May 9, 2012, J.B.'s father directly stated that he expressed a strong preference for 'pure VB-MAPP,' a particular type of ABA methodology. However, at that meeting, J.B.'s future teachers stated that they thought it was best to use multiple methodologies with J.B. A special education teacher stated that she would work off the data submitted by PAC, and then described a number of methodologies she would use with J.B., including natural environment training, things they use in occupational therapy and speech therapy, and various reinforcers and motivators. The principal and the teachers explained that they did not want to specify ABA methodology in the IEP because the teachers wanted to use more than one methodology. As a result, J.B.'s IEP did not specify any particular methodology."

"DOE was not required to specify ABA methodology in J.B.'s IEP. While we recognized in *J.L. v. Mercer Island Sch. Dist.*, 592 F.3d 938, 952, (9th Cir. 2009), that 'school districts should specify a teaching methodology for some students' in their IEPs, we did not provide much guidance beyond stating that doing so is necessary for some students. . . We accord deference to the District's determination and the ALJ's finding that the student's teachers needed flexibility in teaching methodologies because there was not a single methodology that would always be effective. We hold that the District did not commit a procedural violation of the Individuals with Disabilities Education Act by not specifying teaching methodologies in the student's individualized educational programs."

"J.B.'s teachers thought it was best to use multiple teaching methodologies with J.B. They wanted the flexibility to select the methodology that best fit J.B.'s needs as they arose. Given this precedent and the deference we owe to J.B.'s teachers who thought it was best to use multiple teaching methodologies, we hold it was not necessary for J.B.'s IEP to specify that the ABA methodology would be used. Therefore, DOE did not deny J.B. a FAPE and did not violate the IDEA."

Outcome: The school district prevailed.

Return to the Table of Cases

Lisa M. v. Leander Indep. Sch. Dist.
5th Circuit
Judge Higginson
5/15/2019 - Texas

This eligibility case focused on whether the child needed special education, even though it was agreed that the child had a disability.

"When J.M. started fourth grade, his parents asked Leander Independent School District to evaluate him for special education. The District spent weeks analyzing J.M.'s educational profile and determined that he needed special education. Shortly afterwards, following a private staff meeting, the District changed its position. J.M.'s parents pursued administrative relief. A Special Education Hearing Officer found that the school district was right the first time. On appeal, in a comprehensive opinion, the district court also concluded that J.M. was eligible for special education. We affirm."

"The District completed its Full and Individual Evaluation (FIE) on January 4, 2016. The report outlined J.M.'s talents and difficulties, which the District has characterized as a 'varied academic profile.' J.M. was reported to have 'average or near average abilities in the areas of Basic Reading, Reading Fluency, Reading Comprehension, Math Calculation, Math Reasoning, Oral Expression, and Listening Comprehension' but 'apparent deficits in Written Expression.' The FIE also explained that J.M. 'displayed a tendency toward inattentiveness to a significant degree across all settings.' The FIE concluded with a section called 'Recommendations to the ARD Committee.' [Admission, Review, Dismissal] That section included a finding that J.M. met eligibility criteria for IDEA services as a student with an SLD in the area of written expression and with the Other Health Impairment (OHI) of ADHD. Finally, the FIE included a few specific recommendations for the IEP."

"After approximately three and a half hours of discussion, the ARD committee [IEP committee] formalized its determination that J.M. was eligible for special education. The committee memorialized its agreement in a document titled Individualized Education Program (IEP), which certified that J.M. met the criteria for OHI and SLD and, by reason of those disabilities, had a need for special education and related services. The document stated, 'No additional evaluation is needed.' "

"Sometime between the first ARD committee meeting (on January 25) and the reconvened meeting (on February 23), District staff held a 'systematic review,' also called a 'staffing,' at which the District's outside counsel was present. J.M.'s parents were not invited. The record does not clearly reflect how long this staffing lasted but a witness for the District testified that the typical staffing lasts 'between an hour and two.'"

"At the February 23 reconvened ARD meeting, the District informed J.M.'s parents of the District's new position that J.M. was not eligible for special education."

"The parties diverge over what exactly happened at the staffing, and why the District's position changed."

"J.M.'s parents accuse District superiors of 'coaching' the teachers to a finding of no-eligibility through the use of this 'District-only secret meeting.' Regardless, it is undisputed that the District reconvened the ARD committee meeting on February 23 and, at that time, informed J.M.'s parents that the District had determined J.M. was not eligible for special education."

"Shortly after J.M.'s parents received notice that the District considered J.M. ineligible for special education, they requested a due process hearing before an SEHO."

"After a two-day, 20-hour hearing at which fifteen witnesses testified, the SEHO produced a 44-page decision that ruled for J.M.'s parents on the eligibility issue."

"The SEHO found a 'shocking difference' in the opinions expressed by teachers and District staff at the January ARD committee meeting as compared with the February meeting. He determined that the statements made at the January meeting were 'more credible' than those made at the February meeting. And he concluded that 'the evidence establishes a reasonable presumption that District personnel at some level intervened with J.M.'s teachers . . ., either directing or training them to a finding of no eligibility in the February ARDC meeting.' The SEHO ordered the District to convene an ARD committee meeting and 'revise the existing IEP as was planned' for the February ARD committee meeting."

"Pursuant to the IDEA, 20 U.S.C. § 1415(i)(3)(B), J.M.'s parents filed a district court complaint to recover attorneys' fees. The District answered with a general denial and a counterclaim challenging the SEHO's findings of fact, conclusions of law, and relief ordered with respect to the eligibility issue. The parties filed cross-motions for judgment on the administrative record. Ruling for J.M.'s parents, the district court agreed with the SEHO that J.M. met IDEA eligibility criteria."

"The District now appeals the district court's decision. The District concedes that J.M. was a student with a qualifying disability under the IDEA but disputes that J.M. needed special education."

"The only issue before us is whether J.M. needed special education."

"Here, the District concedes that J.M. had the qualifying disabilities of ADHD, DCD, and SLD in the area of Written Expression. The contested issue is the second prong: need. What it means to need special education and related services is not clear. Indeed, one scholar has described this area of law as a 'mess.' Mark C. Weber, *The IDEA Eligibility Mess*, 57 Buff. L. Rev. 83, 84 (2009)."

"The IDEA defines 'special education' as 'specially designed instruction. . . to meet the unique needs of a child with a disability.' 20 U.S.C. § 1401(29). Regulations elaborate that 'specially designed instruction means adapting . . . the content, methodology, or delivery of instruction to address the unique needs of the child that result from the child's disability and to ensure access of the child to the general curriculum, so that the child can meet the educational standards within the jurisdiction of the public agency that apply to all children.' 34 C.F.R. § 300.39(b)(3)."

"Neither the IDEA nor federal regulations define what it means to 'need' special education and related services . . . IDEA and its regulations provide no clues whatsoever to the definition of 'need,' and describing a 'barren' legislative history on the matter. We have had few opportunities to address the question."

"In *Alvin Independent School District v. A.D.*, [503 F.3d 378] we held that courts must consider the "unique facts and circumstances" of each case, including 'parent input, and teacher recommendations, as well as information about the child's physical condition, social or cultural background, and adaptive behavior,' rather than only grades and test scores."

"In D.L., we confirmed that, while grades 'are a consideration in determining whether special education services are necessary,' they should not be the exclusive one.

"The District formalized its eligibility finding at the January 25 ARD committee meeting, which lasted three and a half hours. Nine District staff members participated, including a dyslexia specialist, an occupational therapist, an education diagnostician, an assistant principal, a special education teacher, two general education teachers, and a licensed specialist in student psychology. After detailed discussion of J.M.'s skills and challenges, the ARD committee concluded—unequivocally—that J.M. needed special education. All that remained was to negotiate the details of the IEP. On February 11, the District produced an Addendum to the FIE specifically reaffirming the District's view that 'the student needed special education services.' "

"Finally, the District suggests that 'J.M. cannot need special education because J.M.'s parents have not specified what such special education would consist of.' We reject that argument. A party urging eligibility need not unilaterally identify what the IEP will entail. To the contrary, in Texas, the ARD committee is charged with preparing the IEP."

"The SEHO properly understood and applied the law. . . In sum, the record confirms the district court's finding that J.M. met eligibility criteria for special education."

The Court of Appeals affirmed the District Court's ruling that the child was eligible for special education.

Outcome: Parents prevailed.

Return to the Table of Cases

B.H. v. Manhattan Beach Unif. Sch. Dist.
CA Court of Appeal, 2nd Appellate Dist., 4th Div.
35 Cal. App. 5th 563
Judge Willhite
5/20/2019 - California

[**Wrightslaw Note**: This is not a federal Court of Appeals case, but instead from the appellate court in California.]

"The essence of this appeal is whether a school district may be permitted to avoid its responsibility to provide special education and related services to an eligible student to fund the placement of a child with severe disabilities in a residential treatment center, where that placement was necessary to enable the child to access a meaningful educational benefit, because the child's adoptive parents happened also to have funding available for that residential placement through a noneducational governmental agency program."

"Appellant B.H., a former foster child, has severe disabilities, and is eligible for special education and related services. His adoptive parents (Parents) reside within the geographical boundaries of respondent Manhattan Beach Unified School District (MBUSD). Generally, under the California scheme, the school district in which the parents of the disabled student reside is responsible for preparing an individualized education plan, referred to as an IEP, for the disabled child under the

IDEA, and for paying for the costs of implementing that plan. (Ed. Code, §§ 48200, 56028.) Consistent with this rule, MBUSD prepared an IEP for B.H."

"In the meantime, Parents arranged for B.H.'s placement, later agreed to by MBUSD and consistent with B.H.'s IEP, at a residential treatment center and its affiliated nonpublic school in Sonoma County. They received financial assistance for the placement through the Adoptive Assistance Program (AAP) administered by the Los Angeles County Department of Children and Family Services (DCFS). Such assistance is provided by the federal Adoption Assistance and Child Welfare Act of 1980 (42 U.S.C. § 670 *et seq.*) and implementing provisions of the Welfare and Institutions Code. Parents were entitled to such aid as the adoptive parents of a child formerly under the supervision of DCFS whose special needs preexisted his adoption."

"After learning of the financial aid received by Parents, MBUSD refused to implement B.H.'s IEP and fund his placement in Sonoma County. MBUSD asserted that because Parents received funding through DCFS after the individual education plan was finalized, MBUSD was not responsible for the costs of B.H.'s education. Parents initiated an administrative hearing challenging MBUSD's decision. At issue was whether MBUSD was responsible for paying Parents' transportation costs related to the Sonoma County placement."

"The administrative law judge sided with MBUSD . . . B.H. appealed to the superior court, which agreed with the administrative law judge." B.H. "has now appealed the trial court's decision to this court."

The state appellate court's lengthy legal analysis of the law discussed California's SELPA system.

"All California school districts and county school offices have formed consortiums to provide special education services to children residing within their boundaries. The consortium for each region is called a special education local plan area, referred to by the acronym SELPA.' (*See* Ed. Code, § 56195.7.) An exception to the general rule for determining the responsible LEA is found in Education Code sections 56155 and 56156.4, subdivision (a). Under those provisions, if a disabled child is 'placed in a licensed children's institution . . . by a court, regional center for the developmentally disabled, or *public agency, other than an educational agency*' (Ed. Code, § 56155, italics added), then the 'special education local plan area [SELPA, not the school district of the parents' residence] shall be responsible for providing appropriate education to [children] residing in licensed children's institutions . . . located in the geographical area covered by the local plan.' (Ed. Code, § 56156.4, subd. (a).)"

The Court explained that if there was "some ambiguity in the statutory language, our reading is consistent with the purpose of the legislation. The primary aim of the Education Code is to benefit students and, in interpreting legislation dealing with our educational systems, it must be remembered that the fundamental purpose of such legislation is the welfare of the children. The code must be interpreted reasonably and the court must maintain its focus on what benefits the student, not the school district."

"We reverse. We hold that DCFS is not a 'public agency, other than an educational agency' under Education Code section 56155, that DCFS did not 'place' B.H. in the Sonoma facility by providing AAP assistance, and that therefore Education Code section 56156.4, subdivision (a), did not provide MBUSD with an exception to the rule that the school district of the parents' residence is responsible for the costs of a disabled student's education."

In ruling against Manhattan Beach, the state appellate court relied on a case discussed earlier in this book, (*M.S. v. L.A. Unified School District* (9th Cir. 2019).

Outcome: Parents prevailed.

Return to the Table of Cases

D.L. v. District of Columbia
DC Circuit
Judge Tatel
5/21/2019 - District of Columbia

This is a multi-million dollar attorney fee case that involves issues unique to the U.S. District Court in Washington D.C. and the "matrix" used to calculate fees.

"In this case, after plaintiffs prevailed in a long-running Individuals with Disabilities Education Act class action, the district court accepted the District of Columbia's invitation to rely on the USAO's new matrix in awarding fees. But as we explain below, the new matrix departs from the statutory requirement that reasonable fees be tethered to rates 'prevailing in the community' for the 'kind and quality of services furnished.' 20 U.S.C. § 1415(i)(3)(C)."

"[D]espite plaintiffs' objection that the data underlying the USAO's new matrix incorporates rates for non-litigators outside the District, the court ordered plaintiffs to recalculate their fees using the USAO's rates. Largely as a result of that order (in conjunction with a few minor adjustments unchallenged on appeal), the requested $9.76 million fee dropped to a $6.96 million award. Plaintiffs appeal."

"Simply stated, the question before us is whether the district court abused its discretion in determining that the hourly rates in the USAO's matrix are 'reasonable.' Recall that IDEA makes express a requirement that inheres in any statutory provision for reasonable attorney's fees: such fees must be calculated using 'rates prevailing in the community in which the action or proceeding arose for the kind and quality of services furnished.' "

"Yet here, more than half the data in the USAO's customized dataset comes from outside the District of Columbia, *see* Appellant's Br. 20, and District counsel acknowledges that it includes data from throughout the three neighboring states. Again, it is obvious, as District counsel recognizes, that fees are lower in rural areas than in the District. Indeed, the District's own evidence shows that rates for legal services in the District of Columbia are among the highest anywhere."

"Not so long ago, the prevailing belief was that parties would often be able to agree on reasonable attorney's fees. We regret that this prophecy has gone unfulfilled and fervently hope that practitioners in this circuit—on both the plaintiff and defense sides of the bar—will work together and think creatively about how to produce a reliable assessment of fees charged for complex federal litigation in the District. In the meantime, however, we must discharge our duty to ensure that the adversarial alternative produces results that respect Congress's mandates."

"Because the fee award in this case falls short of that goal, we . . . therefore vacate the award and remand for the district court to recalculate the hourly rate based on evidence that focuses on fees for attorneys practicing complex federal litigation in the District of Columbia."

Outcome: Parents attorneys prevailed. Fee award to be recalculated.

Return to the Table of Cases

C.D. v. Natick Pub. Sch. Dist.
1st Circuit
Judge Lynch
5/22/2019 - Massachusetts

This tuition reimbursement case included issues related to mainstreaming and differing positions of other Courts of Appeal.

The parents challenged "this circuit's prior interpretations of these IDEA requirements as incomplete or as inconsistent with the IDEA and current Supreme Court case law. The parents seek reimbursement for at least three years of C.D.'s education in a specialized private school."

"C.D. has borderline intellectual functioning and significant deficits in language ability. She attended public school in Natick through fifth grade. For middle school, she attended McAuliffe Regional Charter Public School in Framingham, Massachusetts, where she took all of her classes except math in a regular classroom setting. To assist C.D., two private tutors hired by C.D.'s parents attended C.D.'s middle school classes with her."

"The summer before C.D. entered high school, her parents worked with Natick to develop an IEP for C.D.'s ninth grade year at Natick High School. C.D.'s parents wanted C.D. to continue her education in a regular classroom setting, with the help of the same private tutors. School officials explained that only Natick employees were allowed to teach or tutor students in Natick's classrooms."

"Natick was concerned that larger class sizes and more advanced content in high school would make it difficult for C.D. to access the general education curriculum. It considered placing C.D. in replacement classes in which a modified general education curriculum is taught by a special education teacher. Ultimately, Natick, in its proposed IEP, chose a third option."

"The school presented C.D.'s parents with a proposed ninth grade IEP, for the 2012-2013 school year, that placed C.D. in regular classrooms for her elective courses but in a setting called the ACCESS Program for her academic courses. The ACCESS Program is a self-contained special education program located at Natick High School and designed for students who, like C.D., have cognitive and communication deficits. ACCESS offers a significantly modified curriculum, and its students typically earn certificates rather than high school diplomas."

"C.D.'s parents rejected the IEP, saying that the ACCESS Program was an overly 'restricted environment' and that C.D.'s placement there would 'hinder' her academic and social growth. They enrolled C.D. at Learning Prep School, a private school that specializes in educating students with disabilities."

"In 2014, C.D.'s parents filed a complaint with the BSEA seeking reimbursement for C.D.'s tuition at Learning Prep. To qualify for reimbursement, the parents had to show that Natick's IEPs for 2012-2013, 2013-2014, and 2014-2015 'had not made a free appropriate public education available.' After a hearing in May 2015, a BSEA Hearing Officer denied the parents' request for reimbursement. The Hearing Officer concluded that the IEPs were 'reasonably calculated to provide C.D. with a free appropriate public education in the least restrictive environment.' And the Hearing Officer found that the facts and testimony presented did not support the parents' arguments that the transition assessments and plans were inadequate."

C.D.'s parents sought review of the BSEA's decision in federal district court asserting that the school's proposed IEPs did not comply with LRE and that the transition planning was inadequate.

The First Circuit explained that "the BSEA hearing officer appropriately found that the district balanced the benefits of mainstreaming against the restrictions associated with the ACCESS classes, and that the . . . IEPs were reasonably calculated to provide a FAPE in the least restrictive environment possible . . . [and] the district court agreed with the BSEA that the 2012-2013, 2013-2014, and the final 2014-2015 IEPs complied with the IDEA's transition planning and assessment requirements."

"The parents argue, again relying on applications of [the 1989 5th Circuit's decision in] *Daniel R.R.*, that the district court erred in failing to ask whether C.D. could have been educated in the regular classroom considering the whole range of supplemental aids and services."

"The parents frame their claim as presenting the following question, which they say is one of first impression in this circuit: When does a school's decision to educate a child with disabilities in a setting other than the regular classroom violate the IDEA's LRE mandate? Several other circuits, the parents observe, have used the *Daniel R.R.* test to evaluate parents' claims that their children should be mainstreamed. *See Oberti*, 995 F.2d at 1216-17; *T.M.*, 752 F.3d at 161-62; *L.B. ex rel. K.B. v. Nebo Sch. Dist.*, 379 F.3d 966, 976-77 (10th Cir. 2004); *Sacramento City Unified Sch. Dist. v. Rachel H. ex rel. Holland*, 14 F.3d 1398, 1400- 01 (9th Cir.

1994). The parents' premise is incorrect. There is no ground for distinguishing our prior cases, like *Roland M.*, involving parents who sought a more restrictive placement than the one proposed in the IEP. Those cases and this one in fact present the same question: Did the IEP's proposed placement violate the IDEA's LRE mandate?"

"The text of §1412(a)(5)(A) and prior precedent provide the guidance we need to evaluate whether Natick complied with the LRE mandate here. In eschewing the *Daniel R.R.* test because "the Act itself provides enough of a framework," we join the Seventh Circuit. *See Beth B. v. Van Clay*, 282 F.3d 493, 499 (7th Cir. 2002) (declining to adopt the *Daniel R.R.* test)."

"There is no need to add complexity to the LRE mandate in the form of *Daniel R.R.*'s judicial gloss, and every reason not to do so."

"Instead, as we explained in *Roland M. v. Concord School Committee*, 910 F.2d 983 (1st Cir. 1990), 'the desirability of mainstreaming must be weighed in concert with the Act's mandate for educational improvement.' *Id.* at 993."

"C.D.'s parents next argue that the district court ignored the plain language of the IDEA in affirming the BSEA's ruling that the IEPs complied with the statute's transition provision. Not so."

"We have previously held that the IDEA 'does not require a stand-alone transition plan.' Nor does the statute require that the underlying transition assessments take a particular form. Indeed, there is no restriction on the means of gathering information about a student's interests or abilities that may be relevant to the development of postsecondary transition goals. The district court did not err in articulating or applying these transition requirements. It discussed the statute's assessment and planning dimensions, it cited repeatedly to Massachusetts' guidance implementing the federal provision, and it relied on case law correctly applying the transition requirement. The district court then reasonably applied those rules in affirming the BSEA's ruling. The IEPs stated grade-appropriate goals and services designed to prepare C.D. for the post-secondary transition."

The Circuit Court affirmed the rulings of the Hearing Officer and District Court and denied tuition reimbursement to the parents.

Outcome: The school district prevailed.

Return to the Table of Cases

E.S. v. Smith + Montgomery County Pub. Sch.
4th Circuit
5/24/2019 - Maryland

In the procedural predetermination violation case "the parent's alleged that they were not included in planning meetings concerning E.S.'s Individualized Education Program (IEP)... [that it is not] harmless error and must result in the school system providing the requested relief because a FAPE cannot be provided when the parents are excluded from the process. The Appellants assert that a predetermination procedural error per se significantly impedes a parent's right to participate in the decisionmaking process and, therefore, the student could not have received a FAPE."

"The district court concluded that MCPS committed a procedural IDEA violation, and we agree."

"However, it found the noncompliance to be procedural and harmless. It concluded the procedural errors did not deprive E.S. of a FAPE."

In its analysis, the Fourth Circuit explained that "Under § 1415(f)(3)(E)(ii)(II), an ALJ must answer each of the following in the affirmative to find that a procedural violation of the parental rights provisions of the IDEA constitutes a violation of the IDEA: (1) whether the plaintiffs 'alleged a procedural violation,' (2) whether that violation 'significantly impeded the parents' opportunity to participate in the decisionmaking process regarding the provision of a [FAPE] to the parents' child,' and (3) whether the child 'did not receive a [FAPE] as a result."

"Applying this test, we find that the district court

did not err . . . Accordingly, in addition to relying on our recent test outlined in *R.F.*, [*see* the 3/25/2019 case earlier in this book - *R.F. v. Cecil Cty. Pub. Schs.*, 919 F. 3d 237] we affirm for the reasons stated by the district court."

Outcome: School prevailed.

Return to the Table of Cases

J.D. v. Colonial Williamsburg Fdtn.
4th Circuit
925 F. 3d 663
Judge Diaz
5/31/2019 - Virginia

This is a Section 504/ADA allergy discrimination case. While on a school trip, J.D. was not permitted to eat his homemade meal inside a restaurant with his fellow students.

"J.D. is an 11-year-old boy who suffers from several health problems. J.D. experiences a host of symptoms when he ingests gluten, including significant constipation, abdominal pain, foot pain and numbness, cognitive impairment, elevated liver enzymes, and temporary loss of consciousness."

"J.D. is a child on a strict gluten-free diet. In keeping with this diet, he attempted to bring a homemade, gluten-free meal into a restaurant while on a school field trip to Colonial Williamsburg. The restaurant refused to let him do so and offered instead to prepare him a gluten-free meal. But J.D. declined because he didn't trust the restaurant to safely prepare the meal to his specific needs. Ultimately, J.D. chose to eat his homemade meal outside and apart from the rest of his classmates."

"Here, J.D. alleges that he has a disability that prevents him from eating at restaurants. The evidence shows that J.D. repeatedly became sick when exposed to gluten at restaurants, whether from cross-contamination or from human error in following protocols. And this happened despite his parents' best efforts to ensure gluten-free meals."

"In this case, the district court . . . determined that J.D.'s request to bring his homemade meal inside Shields Tavern was not a necessary modification under the ADA because the gluten-free meal offered by Shields Tavern would have provided J.D. with full and equal enjoyment of the restaurant."

"After these events, J.D., by his father and next friend, sued the Colonial Williamsburg Foundation (which owns and operates the restaurant) for violating the Americans with Disability Act, the Rehabilitation Act, and the Virginians with Disabilities Act . . . The district court granted summary judgment to Colonial Williamsburg."

Colonial Williamsburg argued that "J.D. can simply avoid foods that contain gluten. As a result, his impairment doesn't 'substantially limit' a major life activity . . . The district court was required to consider the effects of J.D.'s impairment when he's not on a strict gluten-free diet . . . As the district court observed, J.D. submitted extensive evidence about the serious consequences to his health when he ingests gluten. That J.D. can avoid these symptoms when he maintains a gluten-free diet is immaterial because it runs counter to the clear mandate of the ADAAA. For that reason, we also find unpersuasive those cases pre-dating the ADAAA that considered such mitigating measures."

"Here, J.D. alleges that he has a disability that prevents him from eating at restaurants. The evidence shows that J.D. repeatedly became sick when exposed to gluten at restaurants, whether from cross-contamination or from human error in following protocols. And this happened despite his parents' best efforts to ensure gluten-free meals. At summary judgment, viewing all facts and drawing all inferences in the light most favorable to J.D., we believe there is a genuine dispute on whether eating out is beyond J.D.'s capacity."

"Thus, a jury could reasonably find that requiring the Tavern to allow outside food would fundamentally alter the nature of this service. On the other hand, a jury could reasonably conclude that granting J.D.'s specific request would not have affected the experience of the other patrons in the restaurant. And though food sales are essential to

Shields Tavern's bottom line, there is no evidence that Colonial Williamsburg has been deluged with requests from people seeking to bring in outside food such that it couldn't give individualized attention to the handful of requests that it might receive."

"In short, the question whether granting J.D.'s request would fundamentally alter the nature of Shields Tavern's services may reasonably be resolved in favor of either party."

The Court of Appeals reversed the District Court and remanded it back to that Court for a Jury Trial.

Outcome: Parent prevailed.

Return to the Table of Cases

Donahue v. Kansas Bd. Ed.
10th Circuit
Judge Lucero
6/4/2019 - Kansas

The parent, pro se, filed a request for a due process hearing. The Hearing Officer dismissed the request pursuant to a Notice of Insufficiency filed by the school district. The dismissal was upheld by a Review Officer. The parent appealed to the U.S. District Court, requested a preliminary injunction, and also "filed multiple lawsuits on the same subject matter." She listed as defendants the Hearing Officer, the Review Officer, the Governor, "and officials of the Kansas Division of Child and Family Services (DCF), Danielle Bartelli (an officer of KVC, a company providing child welfare services), and Johnson County District Attorney Stephen Howe."

[**Wrightslaw Note**: The preceding quotes were obtained from the following U.S. District Court cases: 17-2435, 18-2012, and 18-CV-2055 with decisions located in Google Scholar in 2018 on March 6 and 19, June 20, July 9 and 31, August 1 and 27, October 18 and 24, December 6, and in 2019 on January 17 and February 22.]

The IDEA appeal of the insufficiency determination to the U.S. District Court was still pending at the time she appealed the District Court's "denial of her motion for a preliminary injunction." The Tenth Circuit's June 4, 2019 decision is limited to that preliminary injunction appeal. All of the cases against the multiple defendants have been dismissed as to those defendants, except for the local school district, in the IDEA appeal, which remains unresolved.

The Tenth Circuit explained that "The full factual background of this case is not yet before the court, as plaintiff's operative complaint does not contain many allegations. The court has also considered the limited facts it has before it from the underlying administrative proceedings."

"Plaintiff believed that a 'local education agency' (here, defendant Olathe School District USD No. 233) did not meet its obligations under the IDEA with respect to her minor child. She therefore filed a Due Process Complaint under 34 C.F.R. § 300.507. Plaintiff then had a due process hearing conducted by an impartial hearing officer (defendant Lloyd Schwartz), per § 300.511(c). The hearing officer decided against plaintiff."

"Plaintiff appealed pursuant to § 300.514 and Kan. Stat. Ann. § 72-3418(b), and the state review officer (defendant Elena Lincoln) dismissed the appeal as untimely on January 2, 2018. The IDEA allows plaintiff to ask this court to review those decisions. On January 9, 2017, plaintiff initiated this action by filing her Petition for Administrative Review. Plaintiff did not name defendant Olathe School District USD No. 233 until March 20, 2018, in her Second Amended Petition."

"The only proper parties to an IDEA due process hearing are the parents and the local education agency. 20 U.S.C. § 1415(f)(1)(A); Kan. Stat. Ann. § 72-3415(a)(1). Here, those parties are plaintiff and Olathe Unified School District USD No. 233. Defendant Lincoln, as the state review officer, is not a proper party."

"Donahue also filed a motion for a preliminary injunction to protect her and her minor child 'from any present or future action by, inspired by, or initiated by the Kansas Board of Education, Kansas State Department of Education, Olathe School District, or any of the staff or family members of the aforementioned agencies,' including protection from harassment, intimidation, threats, coercion, attempts to have her minor child removed from the home, and protection from all actions while home schooling her minor child."

"On June 20, 2018, the district court entered a comprehensive order that addressed several motions, including the motion for a preliminary injunction. The court dismissed all defendants other than the School District and Swartz as improper parties and denied Donahue's motion for preliminary injunctive relief. The court ordered Donahue to show cause why Swartz should not also be dismissed as an improper party."

"Donahue requested permission from the district court to file an interlocutory appeal from the adverse rulings in the order. The district court denied the request and dismissed the claims against Swartz. Donahue then appealed those orders. We dismissed for lack of jurisdiction because there was no final decision in the district court. *Donahue v. Kan. Bd. of Educ.*, No. 18-3193, order at 2 (10th Cir. Oct. 31, 2018)."

With her second appeal to the Tenth Circuit, the Court of Appeals explained that "Donahue's motion for preliminary injunctive relief was a narrative of her past grievances against school officials, their alleged mistreatment of her minor child, and their efforts to stymie her complaints. She argues that her allegations of past misconduct are adequate to establish irreparable harm, even though she no longer lives in the school district and has not shown an intent to return. But allegations of past harm are inadequate to establish irreparable harm. The purpose of a preliminary injunction is not to remedy past harm but to protect plaintiffs from irreparable injury that will surely result without their issuance."

The Court of Appeals affirmed the District Court's denial of the preliminary injunction.

[**Wrightslaw Note**: On April 13, 2019 Donahue filed her trial brief with the District Court explaining why the insufficiency finding by the Hearing Officer should be reversed. While unrepresented by counsel, she also requested an award of attorney's fees. The school's reply brief requested an award of attorneys' fees against her. She has now appealed that case to the Court of Appeals. It appears that the parent, in the very beginning, either did not consult with an experienced special education attorney, or if she did so, did not follow that person's advice. Per the District Court briefs, many of her pleadings were filed "untimely." Rather than pay for an attorney on behalf of her child, she may now have to pay the school's attorney. She has lost valuable time regarding her child's education and future by litigating worthless claims.]

[Unrelated to this case, Donahue also filed another lawsuit, this time against the Governor of Kansas which was dismissed by the Court of Appeals on July 9, 2019. Click here for the link to that case in this book.]

Outcome: The school district prevailed.

Return to the Table of Cases

E.B. v. Baldwin Park Unif. Sch. Dist.

9th Circuit
6/7/2019 - California

This is a legal procedures case involving judicial discretion, or the lack thereof, and is not specifically related to special education legal issues.

The facts reviewed in the District Court and Court of Appeals files and briefs reveal that the primary special education legal issue was the school's proposed change of the child's educational placement from Kenmore Elementary School to the Cornerstone program at De Anza Elementary School. The school district requested a due process hearing before the Office of Administrative Hearings (OAH) "to determine that their proposed IEP offered FAPE and could be done without parental consent." The ALJ agreed with the school district, ordered the change of placement, and the parents appealed to the District Court and invoked stay-put.

After the Complaint was filed in the District Court, for reasons not clear in the record and unrelated to this case, the parent's attorney was suspended by the State Bar. In advance, he arranged for substitution of counsel. The substitution request was filed with the District Court on June 30, 2017. The Court did not act on the request until October 30, 2017 at which time the request was denied as "No good reason shown." On November 6, 2017 the District Court held a pretrial conference, and no one appeared on behalf of the parents. (Suspended counsel could not appear and there was no new counsel in the case.) The Court, *sue sponte*, on its own motion, ordered the "case dismissed for lack of prosecution." Parents subsequently appealed to the Ninth Circuit.

The Ninth Circuit explained that "The district court abused its discretion in dismissing the action *sua sponte* for lack of prosecution after E.B. did not appear at a pretrial conference. The district court failed to consider less drastic alternatives. In addition, the district court failed to warn E.B. that dismissal was imminent after E.B. missed filing deadlines. The district judge has an obligation to warn the plaintiff that dismissal is imminent. Accordingly, we reverse and remand for further proceedings."

In addition, the Ninth Circuit added that "We grant E.B.'s request to reassign this case to a different district judge. Reassignment is warranted here to preserve the appearance of justice. Thus, we instruct the Clerk of Court for the Central District of California to reassign this case to a different district judge on remand."

Outcome: Parent prevailed.

Return to the Table of Cases

L.G. v. Fayette County Bd. Ed.

6th Circuit
Judge Daughtrey
6/10/2019 - Kentucky

This *Fry* exhaustion case is characteristic of the difficulty in determining when you do and do not need to exhaust administrative remedies.

Without having requested a special education due process hearing, "L.G., a minor, brought suit against the Board of Education of Fayette County, Kentucky, alleging that he was denied equal access to an education in violation of § 504 of the Rehabilitation Act, 29 U.S.C. § 794."

"L.G. has not raised a claim under the IDEA and did not pursue administrative relief prior to filing this lawsuit. The Board contends, however, that L.G. was required to exhaust the IDEA's administrative procedures. L.G. asserts that his complaint seeks relief for the discriminatory denial of access to an education, that this discrimination is distinct from the denial of a FAPE, and that, accordingly, the Supreme Court's decision in *Fry* relieves him of the IDEA's exhaustion requirement."

In the factual background of the case, the Sixth Circuit explained that "In September of 2016, L.G. was diagnosed with an e-coli infection and advised by his physician that he should not attend school. L.G.'s parents alerted the administration at Morton Middle School about L.G.'s condition and his need for an extended absence. At some point between the time following this notification but before late November of 2016, L.G.'s mother learned that L.G.'s notice regarding his condition and inability to return to school was 'not accepted' by the Morton Middle School administration and that L.G. was receiving failing grades due to his non-attendance. On October 5, 2016, a staff member at Morton Middle School reached out to L.G.'s mother offering that she could pick up L.G.'s school work and that some assignments were available online . . . L.G. claims that in the months following his diagnosis his parents were in 'regular contact' with the Morton Middle School staff."

"On November 20, 2016, a social worker from the Cabinet for Health and Family Services contacted L.G. and his family in response to a complaint filed that asserted that L.G. was 'dependent, neglected, or abused.' Around the same time, L.G. and his parents also became aware that someone filed a truancy petition against L.G.'s parents in light of his absences . . . As a result of the complaint and truancy petition, L.G.'s parents were required to meet with a court-designated worker to discuss L.G.'s situation and absence from school. The Board eventually withdrew the truancy charges."

"In January 2017, L.G. was approved for homebound services and, on the 25th of that month, the Board contacted L.G.'s parents about setting up a § 504 educational plan. However, L.G.'s parents removed L.G. from Fayette County Public Schools because of 'the ill-founded truancy charges and the lack of attention to the child's right to an appropriate education.' "

"L.G. filed this lawsuit in state court against the Board alleging discrimination on the basis of L.G.'s disability. The Board removed the case to federal court, and moved to dismiss the complaint . . . [and] argued that L.G. failed to exhaust his administrative remedies."

In addressing the relationship between IDEA, Section 504, and the SCOTUS ruling in *Fry*, the Sixth Circuit provides depth, noting that "The Rehabilitation Act prohibits discrimination against the disabled by recipients of federal funding and requires reasonable accommodations to permit access to such recipient facilities and programs by disabled persons." *Fry v. Napoleon Cmty. Schs.*, 788 F.3d 622, 633 (6th Cir. 2015)"

"The IDEA offers protections to individuals with disabilities from discriminatory treatment and practices, but unlike the Rehabilitation Act, its protections apply only to school-aged children and are focused solely on an educational setting. In many ways, these protections overlap and complement one another, and it is therefore common for individuals who have suffered discrimination in a public-school setting to raise claims alleging violations of both laws."

"But the IDEA and § 504 are not entirely co-extensive, and in some instances, plaintiffs may deem it more appropriate to pursue relief under only one law or the other. However, in the interest of judicial economy and to take advantage of agency expertise, the IDEA requires that a plaintiff exhaust the IDEA's administrative procedures before filing an action under the Americans with Disabilities Act, the Rehabilitation Act, or similar laws when, but only when his suit seeks relief that is also available under the IDEA."

"As the Supreme Court further explained, the only relief available under the IDEA is for the denial of a free appropriate public education (FAPE), which includes instruction tailored to meet a child's unique needs and sufficient supportive services to permit the child to benefit from that instruction. Thus, if a plaintiff raises only a § 504 claim but the discrimination alleged results in a denial of specifically-tailored instruction, or the services necessary to render that instruction meaningful, the plaintiff essentially seeks a FAPE and must exhaust his administrative remedies under the IDEA. If, however, the gravamen of the plaintiff's suit is something other than the denial of the IDEA's core guarantee, a FAPE, the plaintiff may proceed directly into federal court."

The Sixth Circuit, in explaining why L.G. needed to exhaust, said that "Despite his emphasis on the word 'access,' L.G. has not shown that the discrimination he alleges relates to a denial of 'equal access to public facilities' or was otherwise what the Supreme Court referred to as 'simple discrimination.' L.G. does not contend that the school barred his attendance or refused him an aid or amenity—such as a service dog or access ramp or appropriate seating—that would have rendered the facility more available to him. Nor does he contend that these services were available to some students, but not to him because of his specific disability. L.G. does not claim that he was denied support that would be reasonably available to people with disabilities in non-academic settings, or to adults visiting a middle school. Instead, he alleges that the Board failed to assist with his academic needs; that it did not locate and provide educational services for him; and that it ignored his right under state and federal law to access to an education."

"L.G. has not used the words 'individualized education program' and insists that he is not complaining about the lack of a 'free and appropriate public education.' But neither his omission of these phrases nor his use of the word 'access' changes the fact that L.G. is in essence contesting the adequacy of a special education program."

"L.G.'s § 504 claim, in its essence, seeks redress for the denial of what is essentially equivalent to a FAPE. Thus, pursuant to the mandates of the IDEA, he was required to exhaust his administrative remedies before bringing this claim to the district court."

Outcome: School district prevailed.

Return to the Table of Cases

Albright v. Mountain Home Sch. Dist.
8th Circuit
Judge Wollman
6/12/2019 - Arkansas

This is a lengthy decision arising from numerous claims filed over the years in which a District Court commented that "a long history of bad blood has accumulated between Ms. Albright and the District concerning Child Doe's educational needs. The due process complaint that is the subject of the instant appeal, for example, was actually the third such complaint that Ms. Albright filed against the District; the previous two were settled in August 2012 and March 2014, respectively, before their due process hearings occurred. Ms. Albright also filed three more due process complaints against the District after the instant one. While it would probably be impossible to identify any single coup de gras for any remaining shreds of trust or good will between the parties, some strong contenders would likely be Ms. Albright's practice of concealing audio recorders in Child Doe's clothes at school, or the various reports that District personnel have filed with the Arkansas Department of Human Services and the local police department against Ms. Albright."

That lower court evidently also became perturbed with plaintiff's counsel in this and other cases explaining that "Furthermore, the Court finds that Plaintiff has not been diligent in attempting to meet this Court's deadlines. Of the eighteen motions that Plaintiff has filed in this case, eleven of them have sought some sort of extension or continuance of a deadline. *See* Docs. 37, 42, 47, 48, 50, 52, 75, 77, 78, 89, 93. And at least four of those eleven motions for extensions were themselves filed after the deadline at issue had already passed. *See* Docs. 42, 50, 89, 83. Plaintiff's counsel represents that medical emergencies in Plaintiff's counsel's family have made it difficult for her to meet the Court's deadlines in this case."

"[T]he Court estimates that nearly three quarters of the motions that Plaintiff's counsel has filed in cases where she appears before the undersigned have either sought relief from or disregarded this Court's deadlines, or otherwise pertained to untimeliness issues. These motions are remarkable not only for the share they comprise of Plaintiff's counsel's overall motion practice before the undersigned, but also for their sheer objective numerosity: at least 31 such motions in four cases, many of which were opposed and required significant oppositional briefing." [Source - District Court Opinion in Case No. 3:16-cv-3011 issued on July 5, 2017.]

In this case, the Eighth Circuit's opening paragraph explained that "Jacquie Albright alleges that her daughter Child Doe, a young student with autism and significant intellectual deficits, was not provided a free appropriate public education (FAPE) by Mountain Home School District (the District), as required by the Individuals with Disabilities Education Act (IDEA or Act), 20 U.S.C. § 1400 *et seq.* When her administrative challenge was rejected, Albright appealed that decision in federal district court and brought additional claims for constitutional violations under 42 U.S.C. § 1983, disability discrimination and retaliation under § 504 of the Rehabilitation Act, disability discrimination under Title II of the Americans with Disabilities Act (ADA), and violations of Arkansas law. The district court affirmed the administrative decision, granted summary judgment to the District on the remaining federal claims, and then declined to exercise supplemental jurisdiction over Albright's state law claims. We affirm."

The Court then discussed the factual and legal history and noted that "At the close of discovery, the District moved for summary judgment on Counts II through VI. Under local rules, Albright's response was due fourteen days after the District's motion was filed on April 28. Albright moved for leave to file an amended complaint on May 4. The next day, she requested an extension of time to file her summary judgment response, contending that the motion for summary judgment would be moot if the court allowed her to file an amended complaint. The court denied her motion for an extension on May 7. On May 10, Albright requested another extension, asserting that her counsel had obligations in other cases and that her counsel would need to attend to family medical issues over the following weeks. The court denied the motion that same day. On May 22, ten days after the deadline had passed, Albright began filing her summary judgment response, accompanied by a motion to accept her response out of time."

"In its summary judgment order, the district court denied Albright's out-of-time filing request, struck her filings from the record, and granted the District's motion for summary judgment. In her motion to alter or amend the judgment, Albright contended that the court had applied the incorrect standard when evaluating her out-of-time motion. Although the court agreed that it had applied the wrong standard, it concluded that the motion failed under the correct standard. Albright thereafter filed this appeal."

The Court explained that the District Court "did not abuse its discretion in denying Albright's motions prior to the deadline . . . Although Albright's counsel thereafter attempted with some diligence to complete her response, her filing it ten days after the deadline did not create good cause where none previously existed."

"In sum, 'a profoundly toxic lack of trust' between Albright and the District has rendered it nearly impossible for the parties to agree on an education program best suited for Child Doe's needs, despite both parties' seemingly earnest desire to provide just that. Nonetheless, having found no clear error in the district court's factual findings and having given due weight to the hearing officer's credibility determinations, we conclude that Child Doe was not denied a FAPE."

Outcome: School prevailed.

Return to the Table of Cases

C.Q. v. River Springs Charter Schools
9th Circuit
6/12/2019 - California

This is a "stay-put," pendency case in which "River Springs Charter Schools informed C.Q. that River Springs would transfer her to a different school during spring break of her current semester. C.Q. qualifies for protection under the Individuals with Disabilities Education Act (IDEA), and filed a motion with the state administrative agency requesting an order to stay-put at the school she was currently attending, Prentice. After the Administrative Law Judge (ALJ) denied C.Q.'s motion and failed to determine C.Q.'s then-current educational setting, C.Q. filed a complaint in the district court and motion for preliminary injunctive relief requesting Prentice as her stay-put placement. The district court conducted a de novo review of the issue and granted C.Q.'s motion. River Springs timely appealed" to the Ninth Circuit.

"We agree with the district court that C.Q. would suffer irreparable harm in the absence of relief because River Springs intended to transfer her to a new school in the middle of the current semester causing an immediate disruption in her education. The balance of hardships tips in C.Q.'s favor, and the public has an interest in maintaining a child's then-current educational environment while the parties litigate the disputed transfer." The Court affirmed the "issuance of the injunction."

Outcome: Parent prevailed, stay-put applies, District Court ruling affirmed

Return to the Table of Cases

Steven R.F. v. Harrison Sch. Dist. No. 2
10th Circuit
Judge Briscoe
6/12/2019 - Colorado

"In this appeal, Defendant-Appellant Harrison School District No. 2 asks us to reverse the district court's ruling that it violated the Individuals with Disabilities Education Act (IDEA) by failing to provide Plaintiff-Appellee Steven R.F. with a free appropriate public education."

"Steven R.F. is a fourteen-year-old boy with severe autism. In 2013, the District agreed to place Steven at the Alpine Autism Center, a private out-of-district facility in Colorado Springs."

The school district later sought to return the child "to a public school called the School of Excellence (SOE) for the 2014-2015 schoolyear. Steven's mother, Carrie Fernandez (Mother), objected and filed a state complaint asserting various IDEA violations. After an investigation, the State Complaint Officer (SCO) agreed with Mother and issued a written decision (2014 SCO Order). As a remedy, the SCO ordered, among other things, that the District could not change Steven's placement until: (1) staff members from any new placement proposed by the District have observed Steven . . . at Alpine to understand the nature of his educational and behavioral functioning and (2) the District convenes an IEP meeting, facilitated by a neutral facilitator not employed by the School District . . . and develops an IEP that includes a description of placement sufficient to allow Mother to understand what is being proposed.' Steven remained at Alpine for the 2014-2015 and 2015-2016 schoolyears."

Rather than comply with the State Complaint Officer, it did an "end run" and "challenged the SCO decision by filing a due process complaint with the Colorado Office of Administrative Courts pursuant to 20 U.S.C. § 1415(f). The District sought a determination that its proposal to transfer Steven to the SOE for the 2016-2017 schoolyear was an appropriate offer of FAPE. The Administrative Law Judge deciding the complaint concluded that the 'District made an offer of FAPE, and that any procedural violations that may have occurred did not deprive Steven of FAPE or educational benefit, and did not deprive Mother of her right to meaningfully participate in the decision-making process."

"Mother appealed the ALJ's determination to federal district court . . . and asked the district court to find that the 2016-2017 IEP denied Steven the FAPE to which he is entitled. She asserted that the District violated the IDEA by: (1) not complying with the terms of the 2014 SCO Order; (2) not identifying Steven's proposed educational placement (COLA or LIBERTY) in his 2016-2017 IEP; (3) predetermining Steven's placement in the SOE; and (4) creating an IEP not based on Steven's individual needs."

"After merits briefing, the district court concluded that the District had violated the 2014 SCO Order and various procedural protections within the IDEA, and that these violations amounted to the denial of a FAPE. Specifically, the district court ruled, as regards Steven's 2016 IEP: (1) the District failed to include a specific offer of educational placement; (2) the District failed to comply with the requirements of the 2014 SCO Order, which were designed to protect Mother's right to a 'fair IEP meeting,' which includes 'a clear offer of educational placement' and 'meaningful participation in the IEP process,' and (3) taken together, those failures amounted to the denial of a FAPE. The district court ordered the District to reimburse Mother for Steven's tuition at Alpine for 2016-2017 and awarded her attorney's fees as the prevailing party."

"This case concerns Steven's 2016-2017 IEP, which governed a schoolyear that has passed. Although Mother initially sought and was awarded reimbursement for Steven's tuition at Alpine, the parties agree that the District paid for Steven's enrollment at Alpine pursuant to the IDEA's stay-put provision, and need not reimburse Mother for anything. Therefore, unless a mootness exception applies, there is no actual, ongoing controversy before us."

"Because we conclude that the case is moot, we dismiss this appeal, vacate the district court's ruling, and remand with instructions to dismiss as moot."

With regard to entitlement to an award of attorneys' fees to the parent, in a footnote, the Court of Appeals explained that "Mother's argument that equity dictates that we affirm the district court's judgment and remand for a determination of attorney's fees has no support in the law. Under the IDEA, only the 'prevailing party' can be awarded attorney's fees. 20 U.S.C. § 1415(i)(3)(B). A party can only be determined to prevail if it does so on the merits or with 'the necessary judicial imprimatur,' such as through a consent decree. Because the case is moot, the court does not have jurisdiction to make a determination on the merits, and Mother cannot be a 'prevailing party' under the IDEA."

Outcome: Parent prevailed but, because the case is moot, lost the entitlement to attorneys' fees.

Return to the Table of Cases

W.A. v. Hendrick Hudson Cent. Sch. Dist.
2nd Circuit
Judge Hall
6/14/2019 - New York

This tuition reimbursement case involves conflicting decisions between the Hearing Officer and Review Officer and a finding that the private program was not appropriate.

While in the eighth grade, W.E. began suffering from migraine headaches and missed over 100 days of school. "The District eventually classified W.E. as suffering from a disability under the IDEA's 'other health impairment' designation, but the Parents were not satisfied with the individualized education program the District prepared for W.E.'s upcoming ninth-grade school year. The Parents removed W.E. from the District and enrolled him at Northwood School (Northwood), a private school in the Adirondacks, for his ninth- and tenth-grade school years. While at Northwood W.E.'s absences from school diminished significantly, and he experienced notable improvement in his social and academic engagement."

The parents filed two due process hearing requests seeking tuition for each year. Reimbursement was denied by the Independent Hearing Officer (IHO) and subsequent State Review Officer (SRO) in each case, although some compensatory education reimbursement for counseling was ordered.

The "Parents brought these two federal court complaints [and] . . . in Case One, the Parents alleged that the District violated W.E.'s right to a free and appropriate public education (FAPE) for his eighth- and ninth-grade school years (2010-11 and 2011-12) and challenged the SRO's ruling of January 31, 2014, which held that Northwood was not an appropriate placement for ninth grade. In Case Two, the Parents challenged the March 18, 2014 decision of the SRO and asserted that the District violated W.E.'s right to a FAPE for his tenth-grade school year (2012-13); they again sought tuition reimbursement for their unilateral placement of W.E. at Northwood for tenth grade. The two actions were consolidated by the district court."

"[T]he district court affirmed the SRO's ruling in Case One in all respects but declined to defer to the SRO in Case Two, holding instead that Northwood was an appropriate placement during tenth grade and ordering that the District reimburse the Parents for W.E.'s tuition at Northwood for that year . . . vacating the award of compensatory education in the form of counseling reimbursement for the eighth-grade year based on its affirmance of the SRO's ruling that W.E. was not denied a FAPE for that academic year."

"The District appeals the portion of the district court's November 23, 2016 decision and order awarding summary judgment to the Parents and ordering reimbursement of W.E.'s tuition for his private education at Northwood during W.E.'s tenth-grade year . . . The Parents cross-appeal . . . that Northwood was not an appropriate placement for W.E.'s ninth-grade school year so as to entitle the Parents to tuition reimbursement for W.E.'s private education during ninth grade."

The Second Circuit did a comprehensive analysis of the facts and the four decisions, two by the IHO and two by the SRO, and then assessed each case separately.

In this instance of conflicting IHO and SRO decisions, the Court explained that "If the SRO and IHO decisions conflict, the IHO's decision may be afforded diminished weight. In other words, we would defer to the final decision of the state authorities, that is, the SRO's decision. Yet such deference applies only to the SRO's reasoned conclusions—that is, reviewing courts must look to the factors that normally determine whether any particular judgment is persuasive and must ultimately defer to the SRO's decision on matters requiring educational expertise unless the court concludes that the decision was inadequately reasoned, in which case a better-reasoned IHO opinion may be considered instead."

For "Case One: The Eighth- and Ninth-Grade School Years" the Court noted that "Despite the flaws that the district court identified in the SRO's opinion, the court agreed that the Parents did not satisfy their burden of showing that Northwood was an appropriate placement, especially in light of the SRO's analysis regarding Northwood's failure to offer meaningful counseling or vehicles for addressing W.E.'s organizational and stress-related issues."

For "Case Two: The Tenth-Grade School Year . . . [W]e hold that the district court improperly failed to accord deference to the SRO's ruling that Northwood School was not an appropriate placement for W.E.'s tenth-grade year. . . In short, the district court's decision not to defer to the SRO's opinion on the basis of the SRO's putatively perfunctory analysis is not supported by the record."

[**Wrightslaw Note**: Hendrick Hudson was the school district in the famous ***Rowley*** case, the first SCOTUS special education case.]

Outcome: School prevailed.

Return to the Table of Cases

M.G. v. North Hunterdon-Voorhees Reg. High Sch. Dist.

3rd Circuit
Judge Matey
6/20/2019 - New Jersey

This case is primarily about the weight given to testimony from a parent. "Since 2015, the District has provided M.G. services under an IEP. . . Through M.G.'s first year of high school, a program suited to her needs was unavailable within the district. Instead, M.G. attended the Developmental Learning Center (DLC) in Warren, New Jersey. In February 2016, the District issued a new IEP (2016 IEP) requiring M.G. to attend a program in the District beginning with the 2016-17 school year. M.G.'s parents objected to the 2016 IEP and challenged the proposal (2016 IEP Petition) . . ."

"Under the IDEA, that challenge stayed the proposed transfer so M.G. remained enrolled at the DLC for the 2016-17 school year. In April 2017, while the 2016 IEP Petition was pending, the District issued a revised IEP (2017 IEP) and again directed M.G. to attend a program in the District. M.G.'s parents filed a second challenge (2017 IEP Petition) with the Department. As a result of this new petition, M.G. continued to attend DLC during the 2017-18 school year."

"An Administrative Law Judge (ALJ) consolidated the petitions and conducted a three-day hearing in August 2017. As the hearing took place after the 2016-17 school year, the ALJ found the objections to the 2016 IEP moot and reviewed only the 2017 IEP. The ALJ heard testimony from several witnesses, including multiple experts on behalf of both parties. The District's witnesses included a school psychologist; a clinical psychologist and behavior specialist; and the Director of Special Education for the District. Appellants presented the testimony of M.G.'s father, as well as expert testimony from a clinical psychologist."

"Following the hearing, the ALJ dismissed both petitions and concluded that the 2017 IEP provided M.G. with 'significant learning and meaningful educational benefits in light of M.G.'s individual needs and potential.' M.G.'s parents appealed the ALJ's determination in federal court under 20 U.S.C. § 1415(i)(2)(A), and the District Court granted summary judgment for the District. M.G.'s parents timely appealed."

The Third Circuit explained that "The party challenging an administrative decision bears the burden of persuasion and faces the additional hurdle of overcoming a presumption that the Hearing Officer's findings were correct."

"While M.G.'s parents argue that the ALJ failed to give appropriate weight to the testimony of M.G.'s father, they did not present any new evidence to the District Court and relied instead on the record from the administrative hearing. The District Court's review of witnesses, and the weight to accord their testimony, was thus limited to the administrative record. The record reveals no non-testimonial extrinsic evidence that clearly shows that the ALJ was mistaken, so the District Court appropriately deferred to the ALJ's credibility determinations. And the ALJ gave due attention to the concerns M.G.'s father raised about M.G.'s safety and her potential for elopement."

The District Court's opinion noted that "Furthermore, the ALJ discredited M.G.'s father's testimony. The ALJ found that the testimony was not anchored on any competent evidence beyond personal experience to which he gave little weight when determining the appropriateness of an IEP. Additionally, the ALJ referred to D.G.'s testimony as 'sarcastic and other times sardonic', emotionally charged and that he was 'unsparing in his criticism' of the District. The ALJ commented that the thrust of D.G.'s testimony focused on the child's safety, and his fear that M.G. might elope if placed in the District program."

The Court of Appeals upheld the ALJ and District Court's findings, explaining that "Relying on the testimony of the school psychologist, the ALJ determined that the risk of elopement was suitably addressed by the one-to-one aid outlined in the 2017 IEP. There was no error in the District Court's deference to the ALJ's findings."

"For these reasons, we will affirm the District Court's decision."

Outcome: School prevailed.

Return to the Table of Cases

L.J. v. Broward County Sch. Bd.

11th Circuit
Judge Grant
6/26/2019 - Florida

In the opening paragraph, the Eleventh Circuit explains that this case is the culmination of a fifteen-year conflict between the parent and school. The current issue is about the implementation of a "stay-put" IEP versus the content of that IEP.

"Since his third-grade year, L.J.—who has been diagnosed with autism and a speech-and-language impairment—has received special education and related services under the IDEA. L.J.'s path through school has not been a clear one; as early as 2002, his third-grade year, he and his mother have challenged his schools' plans for him, arguing at various times that the plans' content, the plans' implementation, or both, were insufficient."

"The current challenge is related only to implementation—that is, whether and how the school put its plan into action. The question we face is how to ensure that the IDEA's guarantee of a free appropriate public education is honored not only in the content of an IEP, but also in its implementation. And because those two issues—content and implementation—are different in their nature—plan versus action—our analyses of shortfalls in those areas also must be different."

"L.J., a child with autism and a speech-and-language impairment, was a student in the Broward County public school system during his kindergarten, elementary school, and middle school years. During his third-grade year, education professionals at his elementary school worked with L.J.'s mother to develop an individualized education program for him. That IEP remained in place for several years as L.J. progressed through elementary school."

"When L.J. entered middle school three years later, the school board proposed a new IEP that it believed would better suit his needs in the new environment. L.J., meanwhile, strongly disliked the new middle school setting and immediately exhibited a range of problematic behaviors—including persistent refusal to attend school. L.J.'s mother ended up homeschooling him for most of his sixth-grade year, and in August of that year she filed an IDEA complaint challenging the content of the middle school's proposed IEP."

"She also invoked the IDEA's 'stay-put' provision so that the school was required to continue to implement L.J.'s elementary school IEP while her challenge to the proposed middle school IEP progressed through the system."

"Over the fall and spring of L.J.'s sixth-grade year, his mother continued to file complaints challenging various aspects of L.J.'s education, including the school's implementation of his elementary school stay-put IEP."

"[T]he ALJ issued a decision addressing the content of the new IEP and the implementation of the old one; he found both that the content of the proposed middle school IEP was appropriate and that the school had adequately implemented the elementary school stay-put IEP during the challenge. L.J.'s mother appealed from that decision, and a district judge affirmed it. That case and the time period it involved—L.J.'s sixth-grade year—are no longer before us. But because of that case, at all times relevant to this appeal, the school was required to implement L.J.'s elementary school stay-put IEP."

"L.J. returned to his public school for his seventh-grade year, but despite the apparent efforts of both his mother and the school, his attendance problems continued . . . In December of L.J.'s seventh-grade year, his mother filed another IEP challenge—the one that eventually resulted in this appeal. Although the ALJ had found in the first case that the school had adequately implemented the elementary school stay-put IEP through the end of L.J.'s sixth-grade year, L.J.'s mother now alleged that the school had failed to implement that same IEP during the federal judicial proceedings that followed her appeal from the ALJ's order—that is, beginning in seventh grade."

"And so began this case, which relates to the time between the ALJ's decision at the end of L.J.'s sixth-grade year and L.J.'s removal from school partway through eighth grade. Eighteen non-consecutive days of hearings on these new claims spanned over two years between March 2007 and October 2009. Over a year later, the ALJ issued a written opinion concluding that the school had failed to implement L.J.'s elementary school stay-put IEP during his seventh-and eighth-grade years, the time when the decision approving the content of the proposed middle school IEP was being appealed in federal court. . . [T]he ALJ concluded that 'there were substantial or significant provisions of L.J.'s IEP that the School Board failed to implement.'"

"Soon after, both parties cross-moved for judgment on the administrative record. The district court issued an opinion setting the standard of review and ordering supplemental briefing. Five years later, it issued a detailed opinion that addressed each alleged implementation deficiency, relied on an extensive review of the administrative record, and ultimately reversed the ALJ's decision. [On September 28, 2017] the district court entered judgment in favor of the school. L.J.'s mother appealed from that decision, and we now consider whether the school's implementation of L.J.'s elementary school stay-put IEP during his seventh-and eighth-grade school years (up until his removal in the middle of eighth grade) violated the IDEA."

In its analysis of this case, in which testimony was first heard in March 2007, the Circuit Court explained that the 1982 *Rowley* and 2017 *Endrew F.* cases issued by SCOTUS "provide useful guideposts to courts evaluating 'content' claims. But even where an IEP as written may satisfy the IDEA, schools can also fail to meet their obligation to provide a free appropriate public education by failing to implement the IEP in practice. These are 'implementation' cases, and it is this second species of IDEA claim that this case presents."

"We have not yet articulated a legal standard to govern implementation cases. For the courts that have, the heart of this issue has been whether any deviation whatsoever from an IEP necessarily violates the IDEA, and—if not—how far is too far. Confronting this issue for the first time ourselves, we conclude that to prevail in a failure-to-implement case, a plaintiff must demonstrate that the school has materially failed to implement a child's IEP. And to do that, the plaintiff must prove more than a minor or technical gap between the plan and reality; de minimis shortfalls are not enough. A material implementation failure occurs only when a school has failed to implement substantial or significant provisions of a child's IEP."

"Several considerations convince us that a materiality standard—rather than a perfect-implementation requirement—is best suited to determine whether a school has satisfied its obligations under the IDEA, at least with respect to the implementation of an IEP."

"When we consider implementation claims . . . we must decide what it means to provide special education and related services 'in conformity with a child's individualized education program.' And we also must decide what it means to fail at that responsibility."

"The phrase 'in conformity with' suggests that general agreement or congruence, not perfect adherence, is the standard. [Per Webster's] 'Conformity' means 'the condition or fact of being in harmony or agreement; correspondence; congruity; similarity.' Conspicuously absent from this definition are words like 'exact' or 'identical,' suggesting that the IDEA recognizes that some degree of flexibility is necessary in implementing a child's IEP. We see nothing in the text of the IDEA holding schools to a standard of perfect implementation."

"Setting out a standard under which even a de minimis failure to implement a particular provision of an IEP would be actionable would also be inconsistent with the recognition that an IEP is a plan, not a contract . . . To be sure, this is no license for a school to disregard an IEP, in whole or in part, during litigation. But it is a recognition that a properly designed IEP will be capable of providing a free appropriate public education even in the face of a non-material implementation failure."

"We thus conclude that the materiality standard—asking whether a school has failed to implement substantial or significant provisions of the child's IEP—is the appropriate test in a failure-to-implement case."

"We also note that courts should consider implementation as a whole in light of the IEP's overall goals . . . In an implementation case, the question is not whether the school has materially failed to implement an individual provision in isolation, but rather whether the school has materially failed to implement the IEP as a whole. Cumulative analysis is therefore built into the materiality standard itself."

A dissenting Judge provided a lengthy, detailed dissent, noting that "On the merits, I conclude—as did the administrative law judge—that the school board materially failed to implement L.J.'s stay-put IEP in violation of the IDEA."

In a footnote, the Court expressed strong concern "that the pace of litigation in this case was inconsistent with the notion that the most effective means of ensuring disabled children receive an education tailored to meet their specific needs is to provide prompt resolution of disputes over a child's IEP . . . Over two years passed before the ALJ even concluded hearings in this case, and then another fifteen months before the ALJ rendered its decision. The district court had the case for nearly a year before it issued an opinion setting the standard of review and ordering supplemental briefing, and then took over five years to issue its final judgment. As a result, L.J.—now 26 years old—is long gone from the Broward County school system, and any compensatory education he could receive from this case is surely less valuable than it would have been during his middle school years."

Outcome: School prevailed.

Return to the Table of Cases

J.G. v. Hawaii DOE
9th Circuit
6/27/2019 - Hawaii

This is a burden of proof case in which Hawaii wanted to change the last agreed-upon IEP to a new placement and the ALJ, District Court, and Court of Appeals all placed the burden on the parent.

In this relatively short opinion, the Ninth Circuit opened with "J.G.'s parents bear the burden of proof. In cases arising under the Individuals with Disabilities Education Act, "the burden of persuasion lies where it usually falls, upon the party seeking relief." *Schaffer ex rel. Schaffer v. Weast*, 546 U.S. 49, 58 (2005). Although the new IEP changes J.G.'s placement and thereby changes the status quo, J.G.'s parents are challenging the new IEP, meaning they are the 'party seeking relief,' and therefore bear the burden of proof. 'The burden of proof in an administrative hearing challenging an IEP is properly placed upon the party seeking relief. In this case, that party is the student, as represented by his parents.'"

The Court also addressed best, maximizing, and ideal placement vis-à-vis, an appropriate placement. "Last, the record does not show that the new IEP substantively will deny J.G. a free appropriate public education (FAPE). Even accepting J.G.'s parents' arguments about Po'okela's flaws and the progress J.G. has made at the Maui Autism Center, they have not shown that, once an appropriate transition plan is developed, J.G. cannot receive a meaningful educational benefit at Po'okela or that his curriculum cannot be implemented there. *Endrew F. v. Douglas Cty. Sch. Dist.*, 137 S. Ct. 988, 999 (2017) ('The question is whether the IEP is reasonable, not whether the court regards it as ideal.'); ('Appropriate public education does not mean the absolutely best of potential-maximizing education for the individual child.') Moreover, they have not shown that Po'okela is not the least restrictive environment. Accordingly, on this record, we affirm the district court's decision."

Outcome: School prevailed.

Return to the Table of Cases

Jay F. v. Hart Sch. Dist.
9th Circuit
7/1/2019 – California

In this discipline, manifestation determination case, school psychologist Ramirez, who chaired the manifestation hearing asserted that the child's misconduct was not a manifestation of the child's disability. The child was expelled. The parents appealed, requested a special education due process hearing. The ALJ ruled for the parents on some issues and not on others. The parents appealed to the U.S. District Court.

The facts provided in the Ninth Circuit's opinion are minimal and do not clarify the issues. "As the parties are familiar with the facts, we do not recount them here." To better understand the case, we needed to read the California, Central District, Western Division August 2, 2017 opinion by Judge Hatter that was the subject of this appeal. [No. CV 16-05117 TJH (GJSx), Consolidated Case No. CV 16-05226 TJH (GJSx), No. CV 17-00479 TJH (GJSx).] [Scholar.google.com hyperlink is here.]

The child became eligible for an IEP in 2009 when he was evidently in the second grade. The District Court explained that "Starting, at least, in second grade, A.F. was disciplined for serious, threatening behaviors. Those behaviors included threatening and hitting other students, teasing and aggression toward others, emotional outbursts after engaging in behavior incidents, threatening to rape another student, and threats on social networks."

In April, 2015, because of several behavioral incidents that resulted in an expulsion, "A.F. and his father signed an agreement suspending the expulsion [the 'Agreement']. Under the Agreement, A.F. was placed on a 'probationary status subject to revocation by the District's governing board . . . in the event that A.F. violated the District's rules and regulations regarding pupil conduct. [The Agreement provided that] "revocation of the suspension of the expulsion order shall result in expulsion of the Student under the terms of the original expulsion order without the benefit of a hearing."

"On August 25, 2015, two Sequoia students reported to staff that, during the lunch break, A.F. captured a lizard from the side of the building, twisted its neck and broke off its head, and then dropped the carcass on the ground in the presence of other students. A.F. went to the classroom and showed the lizard's blood on his hand to other classmates, who became upset. He told them he did not feel bad about killing the lizard because he was a psychopath. A.F., also, shared the incident with his teacher; showed the dead lizard to another classmate; and told the teacher he was reading 'The Anarchist's Cookbook.'"

As a result of that incident and violation of the "Agreement," he was subsequently expelled. Later, at the due process hearing school psychologist Ramirez said that the August incident was not a manifestation of his disability. The parents arranged for a private psychological evaluation by Dr. Stevenson who "reviewed at least 500 pages of records and met with A.F. three times for a total of about 9-12 hours [and] presented a 29-page abbreviated evaluation report." She explained that "A.F.'s borderline personality disorder necessitates therapeutic intervention specifically tailored to his emotional and mental health needs in the form of dialectical behavioral therapy."

District Court Judge Hatter found that the "ALJ did not thoroughly and carefully analyze whether Ms. Ramirez's determination could be reconciled with A.F.'s extensive history, documented in A.F.'s school records, of making threats dating back to at least the second grade."

He ordered "that the District shall reverse A.F.'s expulsion and expunge any records describing it, specifically the expulsion packet; the alleged stipulated suspended expulsion agreement and the Board approval of that document . . . [and] convene an IEP meeting within 30 days of this Order and develop an IEP for A.F. which provides him with a FAPE. This IEP shall include at least the following components: (1) Comprehensive dialectical behavioral therapy for the 2017-2018 school year; (2) Accurate present levels of performance; and (3) Appropriate goals."

The Ninth Circuit explained that the student's "misconduct was a manifestation of his disability, [and] we also affirm the district court's expungement of Student's expulsion and suspended expulsion agreement resulting from the January 27 misconduct. Therefore, we need not decide the impact of the April 2015 suspended expulsion agreement on Student's rights under the IDEA because it is expunged and legally obsolete."

"The district court did not abuse its discretion in awarding dialectical behavioral therapy as relief for Hart's violations of the IDEA, which authorizes district courts to grant such relief as the court determines is appropriate. The award was appropriate in light of the purpose of the IDEA to provide handicapped children with a free appropriate public education which emphasizes special education and related services designed to meet their unique needs."

The Court upheld the decision of the District Court and award of attorneys' fees.

Outcome: Parent prevailed.

Return to the Table of Cases

R.H. v. Saugerties Cent. Sch. Dist.
2nd Circuit
7/2/2019 – New York

In this tuition reimbursement case, the parents placed their child into The Ridge School, a small private special education school, and sued for tuition reimbursement. The independent hearing officer (IHO) ruled in their favor, but the state level review officer (SRO) reversed. The parents appealed to the U.S. District Court, which upheld the SRO finding that "R.H. failed to meet his burden of establishing the appropriateness of C.H.'s placement at Ridge given the lack of evidence that the private placement was specially designed to meet his unique needs." Parents appealed to the Second Circuit, which discussed the issue of conflicting rulings between an IHO and SRO and necessary proof that a private placement is appropriate.

As with the earlier Ninth Circuit case, this decision provides only minimal facts. "We assume the parties' familiarity with the underlying facts and the record of prior proceedings, to which we refer only as necessary to explain our decision to affirm."

The May 21, 2018 decision from U.S. District Court Sharpe in the Northern District [No. 1:16-cv-551 (GLS/CFH)] explained that "Ridge did not develop any written education plan, behavior plan, or academic goals for C.H."

"In 2014-15, there were four students attending Ridge, including C.H. Two of the students were ninth graders, one was a sixth grader, and C.H. was the only seventh grader. All students were instructed together in all subjects. At Ridge, students did not receive homework, were skipped over if they declined to read in a given subject area, were taught using outdated materials, had changing schedules during their five-hour school day, and were not required to make up work that they failed to complete . . . Ridge employs two full-time teachers and five part-time teachers . . . [and is] an alternative for students suffering from school phobia and deficiencies in focusing, communicating, language processing, and other social skills."

"Moreover, the IHO found that C.H. was making progress academically and emotionally at Ridge. Finally, the IHO found that a balancing of the equities weighed in favor of R.H.'s request for relief."

"Thereafter, the District appealed the decision to an SRO, who sustained the IHO's decision as it related to the District's failure to provide a Free Appropriate Public Education (FAPE) during the 2014-15 school year, but vacated the IHO decision in part, concluding that there was insufficient evidence in the record to conclude that Ridge provided C.H. instruction specially designed to address his social/emotional needs, as opposed to providing a different environment than the one in which he had experienced anxiety."

Judge Sharpe explained that "Generally, if the IHO and SRO reach conflicting conclusions, the court should defer to the SRO's decision . . . the record also reveals that the SRO's conclusion regarding C.H.'s progress at Ridge is sound. Notably, there was scant evidence in the record that constituted objective evidence of progress, which is preferable in this Circuit."

"The record supports the conclusion that R.H. failed to meet his burden of establishing the appropriateness of C.H.'s placement at Ridge given the lack of evidence that the private placement was specially designed to meet his unique needs."

"Accordingly, the District's challenge to the portion of the SRO's decision affirming the IHO's decision that the District failed to offer C.H. a FAPE for the 2014-15 school year is moot and need not be addressed."

The Second Circuit, in affirming Judge Sharpe, explained that "Although there was testimony that C.H. made some progress socially and emotionally, the record contained no evidence of test scores, grades, written behavioral plans, or other progress reports to support R.H.'s claim that C.H. made progress at Ridge."

"R.H. argues that the SRO improperly failed to defer to the Impartial Hearing Officer's expert credibility determinations. But the SRO did not make any adverse credibility findings. The SRO instead denied tuition reimbursement because of gaps in the evidentiary record. For the foregoing reasons and based on our independent review of the hearing record, we conclude that the District Court properly deferred to the SRO's expertise."

Outcome: School prevailed.

Return to the Table of Cases

Brown v. DCPS
DC Circuit
928 F. 3d 1070
Judge Henderson
7/5/2019 – Washington, DC

While this is not an education case, it has law that can impact special education services and settings for children and adults with special needs.

"This litigation began in late 2010, when four disabled individuals filed a class action against the District, alleging that the District's failure to transition them to community-based care violated Title II of the ADA and section 504 of the Rehabilitation Act."

The Court of Appeals for Washington, D.C. explained that "In *Olmstead v. L.C. ex rel. Zimring*, the United States Supreme Court held that the unjustified segregation of disabled individuals in institutions is a form of disability discrimination barred by federal law. 527 U.S. 581 (1999)."

"Consequently, the District of Columbia violates the Americans with Disabilities Act of 1990 and the Rehabilitation Act of 1973 if it cares for a mentally or physically disabled individual in a nursing home notwithstanding, with reasonable modifications to its policies and procedures, it could care for that individual in the community."

In other words, it is a violation of law if the defendant could have cared for an individual in the community by making "reasonable modifications to its policies and procedures."

"This case turns on whether the District can establish that the plaintiffs' requested accommodations are in fact unreasonable, either because the District has an adequate 'Olmstead Plan' in place, in which case every requested accommodation is categorically unreasonable, or because each individual accommodation is so costly that it would be unreasonable to require the District to transfer its limited resources from other disabled individuals."

"The District can meet its burden to establish the requested accommodations are unreasonable in one of two ways. The District can establish that it has a comprehensive, effectively working plan for transitioning the individuals to the community and a waiting list for transition to the community that moves at a reasonable pace, i.e., an adequate Olmstead Plan. If it cannot demonstrate the existence of an adequate Olmstead Plan, the District can establish, seriatim, that each of the four provisions of Plaintiffs' requested injunction would be so costly as to require an unreasonable transfer of the District's limited resources from other disabled individuals."

"The District has not yet demonstrated that it has an adequate Olmstead Plan in place and so has not shown that all requested accommodations are categorically unreasonable. The district court is, of course, free to find on remand that the District now has an adequate Olmstead Plan in place."

"If the District still lacks an adequate Olmstead Plan, its burden is to demonstrate that each accommodation requested by Plaintiffs would be so costly as to require an unreasonable transfer of the District's limited resources from other disabled individuals. Because the district court did not identify this showing as the District's burden, the District did not attempt to meet it. The District will have the opportunity to do so on remand."

Washington, D.C. must prove that it has an adequate Olmstead Plan in place or must show that, to do so, would be financially unreasonable.

[**Wrightslaw Note:** For another case about institutionalizing children, *see* the July 17, 2019 case of the *United States v. Florida*, link here.

Outcome: Adults with disabilities prevailed.

Return to the Table of Cases

Donahue v. Governor Brownback (Kansas)
10th Circuit
Judge Phillips
7/9/2019 – Kansas

The parent filed a pro se case against the Governor of Kansas based on "the treatment her minor child, DCD, received at school. According to Donahue's amended complaint, DCD served 'shock time' in a 5x4 isolation prison cell, located inside his autism classroom, at least six times in a six-month period, which resulted in approximately 65-75 moderate physical injuries, and behavioral and emotional problems."

"Donahue alleged that because Brownback signed the Freedom from Unsafe Restraint and Seclusion Act, Kan. Stat. Ann. § 72-6151 to 72-6158, authorizing the use of such isolation cells in special-needs classrooms, he was liable for DCD's confinement in the cell, which violated DCD's civil rights, the Rehabilitation Act, and the IDEA. She also asserted that Brownback was liable for failing to train and supervise social workers at the Department of Children and Families (DCF), failing to implement policy changes at the DCF, and failing to train police officers in local police departments. She sought monetary damages for herself and DCD, and injunctive relief."

Donahue asserted "claims under 42 U.S.C. § 1983, The Rehabilitation Act of 1974, and the Individuals with Disabilities Education Act (IDEA). The district court dismissed the action for various reasons, including that Eleventh Amendment Immunity barred the official-capacity claims for monetary damages against Brownback. Donahue appeals."

The question before the Tenth Circuit was "whether the district court erred in concluding that Eleventh Amendment immunity bars the official-capacity § 1983 claims for monetary damages against Brownback . . . It is also well-established that official-capacity § 1983 claims against a state official (like former Governor Brownback) are claims against the state . . . It is equally well-established that Congress did not abrogate state Eleventh Amendment immunity when enacting § 1983."

"Exercising jurisdiction under 28 U.S.C. § 1291, we affirm."

Outcome: Kansas and the former Governor prevailed.

[**Wrightslaw Note**: To see the earlier June 4, 2019 case involving Donahue, **click here**.]

Return to the Table of Cases

A.H. v. Colonial Sch. Dist.
3rd Circuit
Judge Smith
7/10/2019 - Delaware

This is a reverse due process Independent Educational Evaluation (IEE) case. In September, 2014, while the student was repeating the second grade, "an Evaluation Summary Report (ESR) was prepared to determine whether Student had a disability under the IDEA and if so, her educational needs."

"The assessment by school psychologist, Emily Klein, based on not only interviews with Student, Parent, teacher, and her own observation, but also a review of Student's record and several assessment tests . . . The tests included the Stanford-Binet Intelligence Scales, 5th Edition (SB-V); the Kaufman Test of Educational Achievement, 2nd edition (KTEA-II); the Behavior Assessment Scale for Children — 2nd Edition (BASC-2); and the Gilliam Asperger's Disorder Scale (GADS)."

[**Wrightslaw Note**: For more about IQ tests, assessment of behavior, reading, writing, arithmetic, and speech/language skills and more, see our book - ***Wrightslaw: All About Tests, 2nd. Ed.*** click here.]

A year later, while in the third grade, the "Student's behavior was problematic with outbursts and conduct that created safety concerns for Student and others present. Two weeks later, Student's behavior was again disruptive and she used a threatening gesture that was accompanied by an oral statement of her intent to kill those present. Student was admitted to the Terry Children's Psychiatric Center and diagnosed with a mood disorder and attention deficit hyperactivity disorder; psychiatric medication was prescribed. After a week, Student was discharged. Arrangements were made for homebound instruction. Student's placement later changed to Southern Elementary School Intensive Learning Center."

"Thereafter, Parent advised Colonial that she disagreed with the September 2014 ESR and requested that the school pay for an IEE assessing Student in the following areas: neuropsychological assessment, occupational therapy, psychiatric assessment, and a functional behavior assessment. Colonial denied the request. In early February 2016, Colonial requested a due process hearing before a Delaware Due Process Hearing Panel. Colonial continued to update its evaluations and assessment of Student's abilities."

At a subsequent due process hearing, the request for an IEE was denied, finding "that Colonial's evaluation of Student was appropriate and that Colonial did not have to bear the expense of the IEE. It considered the IDEA's requirements for conducting educational evaluations and concluded that Colonial's September 2014 ESR complied with those requirements. The Court noted that a variety of tools and strategies had been employed in evaluating Student, which were technically sound instruments. In the Court's view, although the Hearing Panel had improperly relied upon Student's educational progress and the absence of a timely request for the IEE, Colonial had appropriately considered all of Student's assessments and did not rest its decision on a single criterion. *See id.* § 1414(b)(2)(B). The District Court carefully discussed the record evidence regarding the four areas of the IEE requested and explained why the Hearing Panel permissibly concluded that additional testing was not necessary."

The Third Circuit upheld the District Court and Hearing Panel finding that an IEE was not required. For another reverse due process IEE case, see November 14, 2016 *Cobb County School District v. D.B.* case in the Eleventh Circuit where the school district was ordered to fund the IEE and pay in excess of $300,000 in attorneys' fees to the parent's attorney, Jonathan Zimring, who was also counsel in the SCOTUS *Olmstead* case mentioned earlier. The *Cobb County* IEE case is in our 2016 Year in Review book.

Outcome: School prevailed

Return to the Table of Cases

G. v. Fay Sch.
1st Circuit
931 F. 3d 1
Judge Lipez
7/17/2019 – Massachusetts

This ADA, retaliation, private school, expert witness *Daubert* case involves several issues including whether the case became moot. The District Court entered summary judgment for the Fay School against G, who "allegedly suffers from Electromagnetic Hypersensitivity (EHS), a sensitivity to electromagnetic fields (EMFs)." He has "headaches, nausea, nose bleeds, dizziness and heart palpitations when exposed for long periods of time . . . to radio wave radiation emitted from various types of electronic devices, including Wi-Fi transmissions to and from computers."

"In or around 2009, the school installed wireless internet (Wi-Fi), with access points throughout its campus, to allow for increased mobility and flexibility within the classrooms not possible with hardwired devices. The Wi-Fi is frequently accessed by students and teachers at the school. Most upper-level teachers use Google Docs, an internet-based program, as part of classroom instruction. Tablet computers are provided by the school to younger students for in-classroom use, and the school requires that all seventh, eighth, and ninth grade students bring their own laptops or tablets to school for computer based tasks. The students use these devices to access the Fay School's Wi-Fi."

"The family brought suit against Fay after the school refused to remove wireless internet from its classrooms to accommodate G's condition."

"The family filed the operative complaint on February 11, 2016, alleging claims of disability discrimination against the Fay School under Titles III and V of the Americans with Disabilities Act (ADA), which, respectively, prohibit disability discrimination in places of public accommodation, *see* 42 U.S.C. § 12182 (Title III), [ADA link is here] and retaliation for conduct protected under certain provisions of the ADA, including Title III, *see* 42 U.S.C. §§ 12182(a), 12203(a) (Title V)."

At the District Court level, the school filed a motion "in limine to exclude the reports, opinions, and testimony of five of the family's expert witnesses, including Dr. Hubbuch. The family sought to introduce the evidence of Dr. Hubbuch to establish the existence of EHS and to establish G's particular diagnosis. After conducting nine days of '*Daubert*' hearings, *see Daubert v. Merrell Dow Pharm., Inc.*, 509 U.S. 579, 592-93, [SCOTUS *Daubert* case link is here] the district court granted Fay's motion in part, and excluded Dr. Hubbuch's testimony. In so doing, the court explained that the doctor had failed to identify a scientifically reliable basis linking the constellation of symptoms reported by G with EHS in order to 'rule in' that particular diagnosis and had failed to document or testify to her efforts to identify and exclude other environmental factors at the Fay School that might cause or contribute to G's symptoms." *See* also Fed. Rule of Evidence 702(d) requiring that a qualified expert witness's testimony be based on reliable principles and methods properly applied to the facts of the case. [FRE 702 link is here]

[**Wrightslaw Note**: To learn more about the facts, we consulted the District Court's September 29, 2017 ruling at 282 F.Supp.3d 381, and quoted it below. The Fay School District Court link is here.]

"The Plaintiffs failed to produce sufficient evidence to prove that G suffers from EHS caused by Wi-Fi, or was harmed in any way by the School's Wi-Fi system, so Plaintiffs' negligence claim fails on that basis. However, it should also be noted that Defendants correctly argue that assuring that a device is operating within the federally established safety limits as the School did in this case, while it might not satisfy the requirements of the ADA, does fulfill an ordinary duty of care where a Defendant's special needs have not been established." [District Court]

"Taking all the evidence on the record in the light most favorable to the plaintiff, there is insufficient evidence to show specific Wi-Fi-mediated causation. There is sufficient circumstantial evidence for a reasonable jury to find that something at the Fay school was impacting G, and this might be Wi-Fi, but it is impossible to conclude that the evidence on the record would allow a reasonable jury to find that a causal link has been proved without unsupported speculation or brash conjecture." [District Court]

In addition to the allegations that the school violated the ADA, the parents alleged that the school had retaliated against them and their child. The First Circuit explained that "Title V, 42 U.S.C. § 12203(a), prohibits retaliation against an individual who has opposed a practice made unlawful under Title III. The question at issue is what remedies are available to a plaintiff who alleges under Title V that he was retaliated against after opposing a practice made unlawful under Title III."

"By contrast to Titles I or III, Title V does not protect disabled persons in a particular setting; instead, it includes an anti-retaliation provision, 42 U.S.C. § 12203(a)-(b), that protects individuals who exercise their rights under Titles I, II, or III from retaliation. A Title V claim of retaliation thus must allege conduct protected under one of those earlier titles, and a retaliatory response to that protected conduct."

The First Circuit explained that the District Court "granted the school's motion for judgment on the pleadings because (1) it determined that damages are not an available remedy for a Title V retaliation claim premised upon opposition to violations of Title III, and (2) the passage of time had rendered the family's claim for equitable relief moot. The family had sought an order prohibiting the school from retaliating against G, but G had successfully completed the ninth grade (the highest grade that the school offers) at another private school and there was no reasonable anticipation that G would again be a student at the Fay School."

The First Circuit upheld the District Court's dismissal of this case.

Outcome: School prevailed.

Return to the Table of Cases

Edmonds Sch. Dist. v. A.T.
9th Circuit
7/18/2019 - Washington

In this tuition reimbursement case, the Ninth Circuit outlined the issues that must be considered in awarding reimbursement to the parents. Parents prevailed at the due process hearing, both the District Court and the Ninth Circuit affirmed.

The Ninth Circuit explained that "We employ a two-prong test to determine whether a parent or guardian may obtain reimbursement for the costs of private school placement, asking whether (1) the public placement offered by the school district violated the IDEA, and (2) the private school placement was 'proper' under the Act. The district court's equitable decision to order reimbursement is reviewed for abuse of discretion and its findings of fact are reviewed for clear error. We also ensure that the district court gave the administrative hearing officer's factual findings 'due weight,' affording particular deference if those findings are 'thorough and careful.' The district court correctly recognized that the findings in the hearing officer's 57-page decision awarding reimbursement, entered after a six-day hearing in which fifteen witnesses testified, warranted substantial deference here."

"As to whether the placement offered by the District violated the IDEA, the District has not seriously contended that A.T.'s individualized education plan (IEP), which included his educational placement, was 'reasonably calculated to enable him to make progress appropriate in light of the child's circumstances,' as required by the IDEA. Over the course of the two years leading up to A.T.'s enrollment at Provo, A.T.'s grades dropped dramatically, and he received more than twenty formal disciplinary offenses at school, including two emergency expulsions that were later converted to long-term suspensions. Nevertheless, the District did not formally re-evaluate A.T., and his IEP essentially remained the same. Most importantly, the District never offered A.T. a residential placement, despite the fact that, as the hearing officer and then district court later reasonably concluded, residential treatment was clearly necessary for A.T. to function in a school setting."

"The District suggests that A.T.'s truancy rendered him unable to take advantage of the offered educational opportunities, thereby excusing its failure to offer a reasonably calculated IEP. We are skeptical that this could be a valid excuse in any case, but, even if it could be, it is not a valid excuse here. Before A.T. fully stopped attending school, the District had almost two years of A.T.'s performance at school on which to base a new educational plan, as well as a report with an entirely new mental health diagnosis for A.T. The District has also failed to explain why, if locating A.T. for evaluation was truly so important to updating the IEP, it did not attempt to reevaluate him one of the many times that he was incarcerated at the local juvenile facility or hospitalized. As such, the District cannot credibly argue that A.T.'s IEP, and the offered public placement included in that plan, satisfied the IDEA, so the first requirement for reimbursement is met."

"The District primarily challenges the second requirement for reimbursement, contending that Provo was not a 'proper placement' under the IDEA. To be proper, the residential placement must have been (1) necessary for the student to receive benefit from the education and (2) for educational purposes, rather than a response to medical, social, or emotional problems quite apart from the learning process. Both the necessity and purpose of a residential placement are factual findings subject to clear error review. The hearing officer and district court both concluded that, dating to at least the time of his enrollment, A.T. required a residential placement to obtain an educational benefit and that Provo was an appropriate placement under the IDEA."

The award of tuition reimbursement was affirmed.

Outcome: Student prevailed.

Return to the Table of Cases

M.K. v. El Haynes Charter Sch.
DC Circuit
Judge Millett
7/19/2019 – Washington, D.C.

This is a "stay-put" burden of proof and compensatory education case.

The second paragraph of the DC Circuit Court's opinion explains that "The district court in this case wrongly denied a stay-put injunction because it placed the burden of proof on the student rather than the local educational agency. And that error has continuing adverse consequences for the student's claim for compensatory education. For those reasons, we reverse and remand for further proceedings consistent with this opinion."

The opening paragraph explains the purpose and basis of stay-put: "The Individuals with Disabilities Education Act creates a powerful statutory presumption in favor of maintaining the current classroom placement of a student with a disability when the school seeks to change his placement over a parent's objections. 20 U.S.C. § 1415(j). That presumption is commonly known as the 'stay-put' requirement. When a child with a disability has been suspended from school, stay-put heavily favors promptly returning the child to the classroom. As an adjunct to stay-put, the statute also entitles students with disabilities to 'appropriate' remedies like compensatory education to make up for any academic shortfalls that occur during the time they are kept out of school. The local educational agency must overcome a heavy evidentiary burden to displace the default rule that the child will stay-put."

"The purpose of the stay-put command is to strip schools of the unilateral authority they traditionally employed to exclude disabled students from school."

"The School separately argues that this appeal is moot as a result of M.K.'s readmission, combined with the dismissal with prejudice of the School's administrative due process complaint. That argument ignores that the wrongful denial of stay-put not only delayed M.K.'s return to school, but altered his entitlement to compensatory educational services, a claim that remains live in this case."

In other words, since the child, who presented numerous discipline problems, and was later re-admitted, returned to school and subsequently graduated, the case was still alive, not moot, because of the child's entitlement to compensatory education. The Court explained that "In short, because the injury alleged went beyond the ongoing physical exclusion from school and included the educational consequences of his delayed return, the School's belated decision to readmit M.K. did not fully cure his injury, and the consequences of the denial of stay-put continue."

Case remanded and compensatory education to be evaluated. [**Wrightslaw Note**: In 2005, this Court of Appeals issued a landmark compensatory education case, *Reid v. DC*, 401 3d 516 (D.C. Cir. 2005) holding that the DC Public Schools may not be the entity that determines the amount and nature of the compensatory education. Various portions of *Reid* have been quoted and relied on by many courts since then. *Reid* hyperlink is here.]

Outcome: Student prevailed.

Return to the Table of Cases

Anderson v. Abington Hgts. Sch. Dist.
3rd Circuit
Judge Scirica
7/22/2019 – Pennsylvania

This is a discipline, manifestation hearing case with due process hearing, federal court filing, and subsequent settlement. Later the parent and child filed a lawsuit alleging facts related to the earlier discipline incident, evidently believing that they had protected that claim in the settlement agreement.

"On February 24, 2011, the School District developed a suspicion that Jacob was distributing spice, or synthetic marijuana, on school property. The next day, the School District held him in in-school suspension and conducted several interviews with him during the course of the day."

It was "determined that Jacob's behavior was not a manifestation of his disabilities. The School District never informed Ms. Anderson that the school was in the process of making this determination, nor did the School District allow her to contribute to or challenge it." The child "was expelled for the remainder of the 2010-11 school year and for the 2011-12 school year, with instructions to reapply for the 2012-13 school year."

Later the parent requested a special education due process hearing, prevailed, school district appealed to federal court, and then the parties settled the case. After settlement, the parents filed suit in federal court regarding the Section 504 discipline procedural violations by the school district. To fully understand the facts, we reviewed the District Court's December 11, 2017 decision. It explained that the March 31, 2012 decision by the Hearing Officer "found that the District engaged in 'a myriad of procedural and substantive violations' of Plaintiff's rights. Of note, the parties agree that the Defendant's failure to conduct a manifestation hearing and/or Section 504 hearing was fully adjudicated during the initial due process hearing before the Pennsylvania Special Education Hearing Officer. The District appealed the Hearing Officer's decision to the Middle District of Pennsylvania. On August 15, 2012, the parties executed a Release and Settlement Agreement, thereby settling the District's appeal and closing the federal action."

"The District Court found that Jacob's Section 504 violation claim was barred by the terms of the prior settlement agreement . . . Jacob's claim that he was denied a hearing to which he was entitled pursuant to his Section 504 plan is clearly educational in nature and arise[s] out of the Student's 504 plans. It is thus released by the settlement agreement according to the agreement's plain text."

[**Wrightslaw Note**: The December 11, 2017 Pennsylvania U.S. District Court link is here.] The Court of Appeals upheld the District Court dismissal.

Outcome: School prevailed.

Return to the Table of Cases

P.J. v. Connecticut State BOE
2nd Circuit
Judge Livingston
7/25/2019 – Connecticut

This class-action, least restrictive environment (LRE), attorney fee case, began in 1991 and has had a "tortuous history." A settlement agreement in March, 2002 included $675,000.00 in fees and subsequent monitoring. Connecticut appealed the 2017 award of $470,727.57 in attorneys' fees and costs.

"Plaintiffs-Appellees and Intervenors-Plaintiffs-Appellees (collectively, "Plaintiffs-Appellees")—four children with intellectual disabilities, their parents, and several organizations dedicated to vindicating their rights—sued the State of Connecticut in 1991 on behalf of a statewide class of children with intellectual disabilities for, *inter alia*, failing to comply with the requirement in the Individuals with Disabilities Education Act, 20 U.S.C. § 1400 *et seq.*, that children with disabilities be educated in the 'least restrictive environment' that meets their needs."

"The parties negotiated a settlement agreement that included a payment of $675,000 in fees for Plaintiffs-Appellees' counsel. Over the eight-year life of the agreement, Plaintiffs-Appellees took many steps to monitor the State's compliance with the settlement agreement but received no further court-ordered relief in their favor. Near the end of the agreement's term, Plaintiffs-Appellees' counsel moved for additional attorneys' fees, which Defendants-Appellants opposed on several grounds."

Connecticut asserted that the plaintiffs were not entitled to any further fees since the settlement agreement. The district court found "that Plaintiffs-Appellees were not precluded from seeking an award of attorneys' fees and costs beyond the $675,000 obtained under the Settlement Agreement."

The Second Circuit explained that "In determining that the Settlement Agreement did not waive Plaintiffs-Appellees' right to seek future fees and costs, the Magistrate Judge correctly concluded that 'the plain and unambiguous language of the settlement agreement does not manifest an intent to waive plaintiffs' statutory right to seek attorneys' fees.'"

In its review, the court upheld portions of the award by the District Court and reduced the hours in other portions of the attorney fee request. It remanded the case back to the District Court in order to revise the award in light of the guidance from the Court of Appeals.

Outcome: Plaintiffs prevailed, partially, award reduced.

Return to the Table of Cases

LeJeune G. v. Khepera Charter Sch.
3rd Circuit
Judge Rendell
7/25/2019 – Pennsylvania

The parent sued a charter school and the state department of education for payment of private school tuition. While some portions of the desired relief were granted by the District Court, on appeal the parent changed the legal strategy/theory as to the basis for the payment. This case is about appellate procedure.

"LeJeune G., T.T.'s guardian, filed a due process complaint against T.T.'s LEA, Khepera Charter School, alleging that Khepera denied him a FAPE from 2013 to 2015. The officer who presided over the due process hearing agreed and ordered Khepera to provide compensatory education to T.T. . . Khepera and LeJeune G. eventually entered into an agreement implementing the hearing officer's decision."

"The following year, LeJeune G. filed a second due process complaint against Khepera pursuing additional compensatory education and funding for T.T. to attend the Y.A.L.E. School (Y.A.L.E.), a local private school for children with disabilities. . . [Later, the parties] executed a resolution agreement in which Khepera agreed to pay for T.T. to attend Y.A.L.E. for the seventh grade."

"T.T. attended Y.A.L.E. and, by all accounts, was provided with an appropriate education, but Khepera failed to pay all of his tuition" as Khepera became financially insolvent. The parent then "sued Khepera and the Pennsylvania Department of Education (PDE); Khepera was and continues to be financially insolvent, and PDE refused her request."

In her federal court complaint she alleged that Khepera's breach was "a violation of the IDEA and that, because Khepera is unwilling or unable to fulfill its obligations under the IDEA, PDE is responsible for remedying T.T.'s denial of FAPE, including honoring all of the terms of the Due Process Order as interpreted by the T.T. Implementation Agreement and the T.T. Resolution Agreement. This is the only allegation regarding PDE's liability."

"On appeal, Appellant does not rely on the Due Process Award, or the breach of the Implementation Agreement or the Resolution Agreement. Rather, she claims that since the statutory definition of FAPE includes the requirement that an education be 'provided at public expense,' 20 U.S.C. § 1401(9)(A), PDE must pay Y.A.L.E. in order to provide a FAPE."

"This claim was never asserted in her complaint in the District Court. . . This presents a host of issues that were never addressed in the District Court and that were never presented in a way that the District Court could have anticipated them."

"PDE asserts that the precise issue before us was waived as not raised in the District Court . . . it is well established that arguments not raised before the District Court are waived on appeal."

"Appellant concedes that she did not preserve her argument . . . Nowhere were these questions that are implicit in the current argument made by LeJeune G. presented in the context of the litigation before the District Court. Thus, the sole argument presented on appeal has been waived, and we will not disturb the judgment of the District Court."

The Court of Appeals affirmed the District Court ruling in favor of the PA DOE.

Outcome: PA DOE prevailed.

Return to the Table of Cases

Pangerl v. Peoria Unif. Sch. Dist.
9th Circuit
8/6/2019 - Arizona

This is an IEP parental participation and due process procedural timeline errors case.

"T.P. received special education services as student in the Peoria Unified School District. T.P.'s mother, Regina Pangerl, individually and on T.P.'s behalf, appeals from the district court's decision affirming the determination of an Administrative Law Judge (ALJ) that the District did not deny T.P. a free appropriate public education (FAPE) under the Individuals with Disabilities Act (IDEA). We review the district court's factual findings for clear error and its legal conclusions, including whether an individualized education plan (IEP) provides a FAPE, de novo."

Citing *Doug C. v. Hawaii DOE*, 720 F.3d 1038 (9th Cir. 2013) the Ninth Circuit held that "The district court properly concluded that the District did not seriously infringe T.P.'s parents' opportunity to participate in the IEP's creation when it continued the November 29, 2012 IEP meeting for 20 minutes after T.P.'s parents left. Procedural inadequacies constitute a denial of FAPE only if they result in the loss of educational opportunity or seriously infringe parent's opportunity to participate in the IEP formulation process." *Id.* at 1043 (finding a denial of FAPE where the school refused to reschedule an IEP meeting to accommodate an ill parent and completed the IEP entirely without parental input)."

[**Wrightslaw Note**: We have a comprehensive analysis of the *Doug C.* case on our Wrightslaw.com website. *Doug C.* is also the subject of a Wrightslaw Channel YouTube video. The *Doug C.* analysis link is here. The *Doug C.* YouTube video link is here.]

"T.P.'s parents participated in the IEP meeting, with two parental advocates, for over two hours. One of the two advocates announced plans to leave the meeting after two hours due to a personal conflict, but the parents never suggested that they themselves had any conflict that would prevent them from staying. The District's representatives stated clearly that they planned to continue the meeting to finish an IEP that day to ensure that a new IEP was in place before the current IEP expired."

"Parents' advocates acknowledged that they understood that the District planned to complete the IEP that day. The District continued the meeting for 20 minutes after parents left to finish the IEP, and then reconvened with parents later to make changes to the IEP with parents' participation."
"As parents participated in the vast majority of the meeting and then chose to depart, with the knowledge that the District would continue to finish the IEP and without expressing any reason why they could not stay, the continuation of the meeting for 20 additional minutes did not constitute a serious infringement of their right to participate."

Per the District Court's February 17, 2017 decision "Plaintiff claims that the ALJ issued his Decision 159 days after the conclusion of the hearing and 427 days after the filing of the Due Process Complaint in violation of IDEA's 75-day procedural safeguard." The Ninth Circuit noted that the "district court properly concluded that the ALJ's late issuance of his decision, in violation of the IDEA's requirement that a final decision be issued within 75 days of the filing of a complain, did not deny T.P. a FAPE. While the decision was concededly late, this is a procedural error, and, as appellants presented no evidence that it resulted in the loss of any educational opportunity, it is not a denial of a FAPE. *See Doug C.*, 720 F.3d at 1043."

The Ninth Circuit affirmed the District Court ruling in favor of the school district.

Outcome: School prevailed.

Return to the Table of Cases

Parent/Professional Advoc League, Disability Law Center, MW v. Springfield Pub. Sch.
1st Circuit
934 F.3d 13 (2019)
Judge Lynch
8/8/2019 - Massachusetts

This Fry "exhaustion" case is about "standing" to bring a lawsuit, certification of a class, and the "overlap between Title II of the Americans with Disabilities Act (ADA), 42 U.S.C. §§ 12131-12134, and the Individuals with Disabilities Education Act (IDEA), 20 U.S.C. § 1400 *et seq.*"

"The underlying suit alleges that the City of Springfield, Massachusetts, and Springfield Public Schools (SPS) violated Title II of the ADA by unnecessarily segregating students with mental health disabilities in a separate and inferior school, the Springfield Public Day School (SPDS). S.S., then an SPDS student, brought the suit on his own behalf and on behalf of a class of all students with a mental health disability who are or have been enrolled at SPDS. Two associations, the Parent/Professional Advocacy League (PPAL) and Disability Law Center (DLC), joined S.S. as plaintiffs. They seek injunctive and declaratory relief, including an order that defendants provide the class plaintiffs with school-based behavior services in neighborhood schools to afford them an equal educational opportunity and enable them to be educated in neighborhood schools."

"The plaintiffs' consolidated appeal challenges the district court's rulings that this suit was subject to the IDEA's exhaustion requirement and that the proposed class did not satisfy Federal Rule of Civil Procedure 23(a)'s requirements for certification." [FRCP Rule 23 link is here.]

"Title II of the ADA states that 'no qualified individual with a disability shall, by reason of such disability, be excluded from participation in or be denied the benefits of the services, programs, or activities of a public entity, or be subjected to discrimination by any such entity.' 42 U.S.C. § 12132. Title II's regulations generally require a public entity to make 'reasonable modifications' to its 'policies, practices, or procedures' when necessary to avoid violations of Title II. 28 C.F.R. § 35.130(b)(7)(i)." [ADA statute/USC link is here. ADA regulation/CFR link is here.]

"Title II, as implemented by regulation, prohibits two types of discrimination relevant here. First, regulations implementing Title II prohibit inequality in services, programs, or activities provided by public entities. Public entities may not '[a]fford a qualified individual with a disability an opportunity to participate in or benefit from the aid, benefit or service that is not equal to that afforded others' or '[p]rovide a qualified individual with a disability with an aid, benefit or service that is not as effective in affording equal opportunity to obtain the same result, to gain the same benefit, or to reach the same level of achievement as that provided to others.' *Id.* §§ 35.130(b)(1)(ii)-(iii)."

"Second, the regulations require public entities to 'administer services, programs, and activities in the most integrated setting appropriate to the needs of qualified individuals with disabilities.' *Id.* § 35.130(d). 'The most integrated setting' is defined as a setting that 'enables individuals with disabilities to interact with nondisabled persons to the fullest extent possible.' *Id.* pt. 35, app. B."

"Interpreting Title II and the integration and reasonable modification regulations, the Supreme Court held in *Olmstead v. L.C. ex rel. Zimring*, 527 U.S. 581 (1999), that the ADA prohibits the unjustified institutionalization of people with mental disabilities. *Id.* at 600. The Court concluded that public entities must provide 'community-based [services] for persons with mental disabilities,' when 'the affected persons do not oppose such' services, and the community placement 'can be reasonably accommodated.' *Id.* at 607. Cases like this one challenging the separation of individuals with disabilities under the ADA are often called *Olmstead* cases."

"SPS, the second largest school district in Massachusetts, enrolls around 26,000 students in about fifty schools. Most of those schools are neighborhood schools — elementary and middle schools that enroll students based on their residential addresses and high schools that enroll students through a choice program. Within SPS, SPDS comprises three schools, an elementary, middle, and high school. SPDS operates as an alternative set of schools for students with social emotional behavioral disabilities. It enrolls about 230 students, each of whom has been diagnosed with a mental health disability that SPS has determined interferes with his or her learning and each of whom has an IEP that places him or her at SPDS. About 400 other students with mental health disabilities that similarly interfere with their learning attend neighborhood schools; their IEPs do not require placement at SPDS."

"The complaint alleges that both Springfield and SPS discriminate against the plaintiff class under Title II by providing unequal educational services at SPDS and by denying them the opportunity to receive educational services in the most integrated setting appropriate to their needs."

The issue then was whether this was an ADA *Olmstead* type of case or an IDEA least restrictive environment LRE case.

Under IDEA, "every IEP must specify the extent, if any, to which the child will not participate with nondisabled children in the regular class. This requirement reflects the state's obligation to educate children in the LRE . . . To the maximum extent appropriate, children with disabilities . . . are educated with children who are not disabled, and special classes, separate schooling, or other removal of children with disabilities from the regular educational environment occurs only when the nature or severity of the disability of a child is such that education in regular classes with the use of supplementary aids and services cannot be achieved satisfactorily."

"*Fry* recognized that the same conduct might violate both the ADA and the IDEA . . . On inspection, the complaint here in essence contests the provision of educational services secured by the IDEA; its gravamen is not simple discrimination."

"On its surface, the complaint pleads disability-based discrimination: it alleges that the defendants are violating the ADA by unnecessarily segregating students with mental health disabilities in a separate and unequal educational program. And the complaint never uses the term FAPE. Yet, the crux of the complaint is that the defendants failed to provide the educational instruction and related services that the class plaintiffs need to access an appropriate education in an appropriate environment. That is not a claim of simple discrimination; it is a claim contesting the adequacy of a special education program."

"The complaint's gravamen is also revealed in the legal allegations. The sole count of the complaint alleges that the defendants are denying students the opportunity to receive educational programs and services in the most integrated setting appropriate to their needs. And Count I also alleges that the school system is denying students the opportunity to benefit from educational services. These allegations track the language of the ADA's regulations, *see* 28 C.F.R. §§ 35.130(b), (d), but they are nonetheless claims about obligations under the IDEA to educate students in the regular classroom with their nondisabled peers 'to the maximum extent appropriate,' 20 U.S.C. § 1412(a)(5)(A), and to offer students an appropriate educational benefit. These allegations are, in great part, simply another way of saying, in IDEA terms, that the school system has not provided the necessary special educational services to allow students to be educated in the LRE. Indeed, here, the members of the class were placed in SPDS by their IEPs, which, as we outlined above, must provide an appropriate education and must comport with the IDEA's LRE requirement."

"Applying *Fry* for the first time in this circuit, we conclude that the complaint 'seeks relief that is also available' under the IDEA."

The Court upheld the District Court's dismissal for failure to exhaust administrative remedies.

With regard to certification of the class, the "district court also concluded that the plaintiffs had not satisfied Federal Rule of Civil Procedure 23(a)'s prerequisites for class certification. There was no 'question of law or fact common to the class,' the district court held, and S.S. could not serve as a typical or adequate class representative because he had exhausted his IDEA administrative remedies while other class members had not."

The First Circuit provided an extensive discussion about class certification and exhaustion by one or more members of the potential class and then affirmed the District Court's finding that the class could not be certified for class action lawsuit.

With regard to the standing of the two organizations to bring a lawsuit on behalf of a class, the District Court held that they did not have standing. On appeal to the First Circuit, this Court explained that the two groups seek "to sue on behalf of hundreds of children who have not chosen to sue or even to pursue related administrative remedies. The complaint, as we have explained in our analysis of exhaustion and commonality, concerns multiple facets of each child's special education program. The suit thus raises concerns about representativeness. And, in its scale and complexity, the suit poses challenges of judicial administration and efficiency not present in more run-of-the-mill proceedings that Congress might have envisioned."

It added that "adjudication of the claims here would turn on facts specific to each student, including unique features of each student's unique disability, needs, services, and placement. Efficient and successful judicial resolution of the claims would thus require participation and cooperation by numerous students and parents. And, as we stated, representative standing is inappropriate where such participation is necessary."

The Court affirmed the ruling that the two groups did not have standing to bring the lawsuit.

The Court affirmed the District Court's dismissal of this case.

Outcome: School district prevailed.

Return to Table of Cases

W.V. v. Copperas Cove Indep. Sch. Dist.
5th Circuit
8/8/2019 - Texas

This is an eligibility determination case marred by a District Court's failure to "apply the complete standard [and] . . . make underlying factual findings."

The Fifth Circuit explained that "IDEA does not compel the School District to provide a student with an Individualized Education Program unless the student qualifies as a 'child with a disability' under the Act. There is a two-part test for making that determination: A child qualifies as a 'child with a disability' under the IDEA if the child (1) has an intellectual disability, specific learning disability, or other health impairment and, (2) 'by reason thereof, needs special education and related services.' The district court concluded that the plaintiffs' son meets the definition simply because dyslexia qualifies as a specific learning disability. It failed to engage with the second part of the test—namely, whether the plaintiffs' son needs special education."

"Because the district court did not apply the second part of the test, it did not consider whether the accommodations being provided to the plaintiffs' son constitute 'special education' or instead only 'related services. The court also made no findings as to whether the plaintiffs' son was making progress under the accommodations he was receiving. Consideration of those questions might lead the district court to reach a different conclusion on the child's eligibility for an Individualized Education Program, or on the issue of whether the School District's current accommodations were adequate to meet the child's educational needs."

"In IDEA cases, a district court must receive the records of the administrative proceedings and, basing its decision on the preponderance of the evidence, grant such relief as the court determines is appropriate. On appeal, we review the district court's decision as a mixed question of law and fact. While the district court's legal conclusions are reviewed de novo, its factual findings are entitled to clear error deference."

"The record before us does not permit meaningful appellate review; because the district court did not apply the complete standard, it did not make underlying factual findings the review of which is necessary for us to conclude that its legal conclusions were correct. Accordingly, we VACATE and REMAND for reconsideration in light of the appropriate standard."

Outcome: Decision vacated and remanded. Neither party prevailed.

[**Wrightslaw Note**: Texas attorney, Roy T. Attwood participated in this case by filing an amicus, "friend of the court" brief. Roy advised that, on remand, the District Court judge held that, even though "the student did require specially designed instruction, [he] still found for the District. The case is now pending again before the Fifth Circuit." Roy helped us edit this book.]

Return to Table of Cases

Paul G. v. Monterey Peninsula Unif. Sch. Dist. + CA DOE
9th Circuit
933 F.3d 1096
Judge Schroeder
8/12/2019 – California

This is a *Fry* "exhaustion" case about Paul and "a sad story of failed attempts to place him in an appropriate educational facility . . . During his junior year in high school (2014-15), he began having episodes of violent and threatening behavior towards the school staff and fellow students. After unsuccessful efforts to provide instruction at home and in the local library, the school district in July of 2015 held an Individualized Education Plan (IEP) meeting and offered to place Paul in a residential facility. Because he was by then 18 years old, however, no residential facility in the state would accept him. Paul subsequently enrolled in a residential facility in Kansas, but became homesick and returned to California."

"Paul's counsel initiated IDEA administrative proceedings in August 2015, seeking a due process hearing with the California Office of Administrative Hearings (OAH). His complaint alleged he had been denied a FAPE guaranteed under the IDEA. He sought a residential placement in California, monetary damages, and an order directing the California Department of Education ("CDE") and the school district to develop in-state residential placements for adult students like Paul."

"OAH dismissed the claims against the state, ruling that the agency did not have jurisdiction to order the creation of facilities for students over 18, and that the school district, not the state, was responsible for education decisions affecting Paul. Paul then entered into a settlement agreement with the school district in which OAH dismissed the case without ever ruling on his claim that the lack of an in-state residential facility had denied him a FAPE."

"Paul filed this action in federal court in September 2016, following the settlement with the school district. His complaint alleged that CDE violated the Rehabilitation Act and the ADA. The gravamen of his complaint was that to receive a FAPE he required a residential placement, and the state had failed to provide him one in California."

"Paul's position is that California has unlawfully discriminated against him by not providing a residential educational facility for adult students in the state who, like Paul, require such a facility in order to receive a FAPE. He argues he need not exhaust because his claims seek relief for disability discrimination and that even if his claims do involve denial of a FAPE, they fall under the exhaustion exceptions."

"He now argues it would have been futile to pursue the IDEA claim because the state could not be required to provide the facility."

"The district court understood that because Paul's claim is that an in-state residential institution is necessary for him to receive the education guaranteed under the IDEA, he must exhaust his administrative remedies for an IEP. Applying *Fry*, the district court held that the 'alleged denial to provide an in-state residential treatment facility applies solely in a school setting' and the fact that Paul 'previously pursued an IDEA administrative proceeding based on identical or similar allegations supports the conclusion that his claims are premised on a denial of a FAPE.' We agree with that conclusion."

The Court of Appeals upheld the District Court's dismissal based on the failure to exhaust administrative remedies.

Outcome: The State DOE prevailed.

Return to Table of Cases

Doucette v. Georgetown Pub. Sch.
1st Circuit
936 F.3d 16
Judge Lipez
8/26/2019 – Massachusetts

This is a "service dog" *Fry* exhaustion case with facts quite similar to *Fry*. The Court of Appeals opened this case by explaining that the parents "alleged that the school district deprived B.D. of his service animal and subjected him to a dangerous environment in violation of federal and state law, thereby causing B.D. to experience seizures and hospitalization. They sought money damages for alleged permanent physical and emotional harm to B.D., as well as for loss of consortium to the parents."

"Agreeing that the Doucettes' federal claims were subject to the IDEA's exhaustion requirement, the district court granted the school district's motion as to those claims and remanded the Doucettes' state law claims to state court."

"B.D. attended Perley Elementary School (Perley) from July 2009 until August 2012, when he was between the ages of three and six years old. Given his disabilities, he had an individualized education program (IEP), which required, among other things, that he receive a consistent routine, a seizure plan, and one-on-one assistance, and that he participate in an extended-school year (ESY) program."

"B.D.'s parents were dissatisfied with the services provided to B.D. at Perley. Within months of his arrival, they began complaining to administrators, teachers, and the superintendent. In the spring, they met with his IEP team to formally request a change to B.D.'s IEP, which was denied. In the weeks that followed, they continued to convey concerns, noting that B.D. was at times unsupervised, was bolting from class, and, on one occasion, fell and hit his head."

"During the 2010-2011 school year, the Doucettes continued to be dissatisfied with the implementation of B.D.'s IEP. B.D. began having 'staring spells with eye rolling,' symptomatic of potential seizure activity. And, although B.D.'s amended IEP included a safety and seizure plan, one of B.D.'s teachers indicated to B.D.'s mother that she was unaware of the plan."

"In the fall of 2011, B.D. began working with a certified service dog that assisted him with his anxiety and balance, and alerted his caretakers to an impending seizure. In November of that year, the Doucettes requested that the school district permit the dog to accompany B.D. at school as a disability accommodation. The school district refused. When B.D.'s staring spells and anxiety increased, however, the school district offered him at-school access to the service animal if the Doucettes agreed to a school policy regarding the dog's handling. The Doucettes refused to sign this agreement, which they claim violated the Americans with Disabilities Act (ADA). They demanded that the district comply with the ADA. The school district then denied B.D. access to the dog but ordered a behavioral assessment, to take place the next fall (i.e., fall of 2012), to determine whether B.D.'s IEP should be amended to include the service dog."

"In the following weeks, B.D. suffered two more tonic-clonic seizures, each requiring a hospital stay. After the fourth seizure, the Doucettes removed B.D. from school and again requested an alternative school placement. They explained that 'B.D. had had four tonic-clonic seizures in his lifetime, all of which happened in school in the last month,' and that B.D.'s placement was not only inappropriate but unsafe. They also presented the school district with a letter from B.D.'s doctor stating that the current placement was inadequate in terms of managing B.D.'s seizures,; expressing concerns regarding the school's ability to handle B.D.'s health and safety, and recommending, given the severity of B.D.'s anxiety in his then classroom setting, and the subsequent effect on his epilepsy and overall health, that B.D. be kept out of school until a safe placement was identified. Still, the school district refused to provide an alternative placement for B.D. and advised the Doucettes that B.D. was expected to attend school on September 5, 2012, and that extended absences would be considered truancy."

"On September 5, 2012, the Doucettes returned B.D. to Perley. That same day, he suffered a fifth tonic-clonic seizure, requiring hospitalization. After the fifth seizure in a three-month period, the school district agreed to evaluate an out-of-district placement for B.D. Subsequently, the district agreed to the new placement, where B.D. has made developmental and educational progress. B.D. has experienced no seizures since his removal from the school district."

"The Doucettes allege that the school district violated section 504 by refusing to permit B.D. access to his service dog . . . despite having knowledge that B.D. qualified as an individual with disabilities who relied upon the service dog. They assert that B.D. suffered life-threatening seizures because of the deprivation, and they seek money damages for associated medical costs."

"The Doucettes' § 1983 claim is premised on an alleged violation of B.D.'s substantive due process rights secured by the Fourteenth Amendment. The Doucettes allege that these rights were violated during the summer and fall of 2012 when the school district, despite having actual notice that Georgetown Public Schools was an inappropriate placement for B.D., refused to allow an in-district or out-of-district placement and threatened the Doucettes with truancy in the event of any extended absences. They assert that this conduct amounted to deliberate indifference and severe, pervasive disregard for the safety and well-being of B.D. and that, as a result, B.D. suffered great physical and emotional harm, including five life-threatening tonic-clonic seizures."

"The gravamen of this claim — B.D., a disabled child, was denied access to his seizure-alert service dog, and, as a result, suffered seizures — is not the denial of a FAPE. Instead, it is 'simple discrimination, irrespective of the IDEA's FAPE obligation.' *Fry*, 137 S. Ct. at 756. In reaching this conclusion, we 'attend to the diverse means and ends of . . . the IDEA . . . and the Rehabilitation Act . . . The IDEA guarantees individually tailored educational services, while . . . section 504 promises non-discriminatory access to public institutions, . . . sometimes by means of reasonable accommodations.' To be sure, there is some overlap in coverage between the statutes. But here the section 504 claim, grounded in the refusal of the school district to reasonably accommodate B.D.'s use of the service dog, that is the allegation, involves the denial of non-discriminatory access to a public institution, irrespective of the school district's FAPE obligation to provide a particular education program for B.D."

"We conclude that (1) exhaustion was not required

for the Doucettes' section 504 claim because the crux of the claim is not the denial of a FAPE; and (2) although the crux of the Doucettes' § 1983 claim is the denial of a FAPE, that claim is properly brought in federal court because it either was exhausted or further invocation of the administrative process would have been futile."

Reversed and remanded back to the District Court.

[**Wrightslaw Note**: This case was initially filed in state court and, as noted in the beginning, is markedly similar to the SCOTUS *Fry* decision issued in 2017. Since a "Federal Question" was involved, the defendant had the absolute right to remove the case to federal court, which was done with the **original *Doucette* state court complaint** located on the Wrightslaw website, click here. After the First Circuit issued this decision, pursuant to FRAP 35, the defendants requested a Rehearing En Banc, i.e., to be heard by the full court. That Petition was denied on November 25, 2019. The case was remanded back to the U.S. District Court and is now pending. On January 9, 2020 that Court issued an Order for a Status Conference to be held on July 10, 2020. Typically issues such as discovery, jury instructions and timelines will be discussed, if the case is not settled by then.

Outcome: Parent prevailed.

Return to Table of Cases

Wilson v. Southlake Police Dept.
5th Circuit
936 F. 3d 326
Judge Graves
8/28/2019 - Texas

In this Section 504/ADA case regarding S.W., an eight-year old child with autism, School Resource Officer (SRO) Baker "handcuffed S.W. and took him to Wagnon's office. Baker sat face-to-face with S.W., screamed at him, called him names, including punk and brat, mocked S.W., and laughed at him." As a part of that incident, S. W. had a jump rope, that he referred to as his nunchucks and "twirled the jump rope and attempted to hit [Principal] Wagnon. He also threw a cup of coffee and hit the wall."

"Baker continued antagonizing S.W. and aggravating the situation until S.W.'s parents arrived. When S.W.'s mother asked Baker if he realized handcuffing a child with autism would traumatize him, Baker replied: 'You know what? You're right, I don't know that. I'm not a psychologist.' With regard to S.W. having autism, Baker said, 'You know what, he has no sign on his head that says, 'I have autism, I hit people.' You can't do that in a free society.' Baker then continued to laugh and make comments like 'Great parenting!' S.W.'s mother yelled at Baker for laughing and asked for his information. Baker then demanded that they leave the school. S.W. was being carried by his father as they left the school. As a result of this incident, Baker filed various criminal charges against S.W."

"The record indicates that Baker was never properly trained to handle such situations. However, the agreement between the City and Carroll ISD [regarding SROs] provided that Baker would be informed of the need for any special accommodations and would be properly trained to deal with such issues. Any violation of that agreement was not the fault or responsibility of S.W."

"An internal affairs investigation found that Baker's interaction with S.W. was unprofessional and unreasonable. Further, Baker's conduct was demeaning, berating and antagonizing toward S.W. Baker was terminated by the City as a result."

S.W.'s parents, individually and as next friend for S.W., filed suit against the City of Southlake, the Southlake Police Department, and Randy Baker, alleging violations of the Americans with Disability Act of 1990, Section 504 of the Rehabilitation Act of 1973, and constitutional claims pursuant to 42 U.S.C. § 1983. The defendants filed a motion to dismiss, or in the alternative, for summary judgment. The district court subsequently granted the motion. Now S.W. appeals the dismissal of the disability discrimination claims pursuant to a summary judgment standard."

The Court of Appeals explained that "Title II of the ADA provides that 'no qualified individual with a disability shall, by reason of such disability, be excluded from participation in or be denied the benefits of the services, programs, or activities of a public entity, or be subjected to discrimination by any such entity." 42 U.S.C. § 12132.

"This court has said that the evaluation of a claim for disability discrimination under the ADA and the Rehabilitation Act are substantially the same and the only material difference between the two provisions lies in their respective causation requirements. Under Section 504, the plaintiff must establish that disability discrimination was the sole reason for the exclusion or denial of benefits., while under Title II of the ADA, discrimination need not be the sole reason."

"Here, we have an eight-year-old child with disabilities known to the officer and in possession of a child's jump rope provided by the school. There was no potentially life-threatening situation or threat to human life. As the district court stated, this was merely a disruption."

"A jump rope in the hands of an eight-year-old child is not a weapon and is not capable of inflicting the same injuries or damage as an actual weapon, such as nunchucks, in the hands of an adult. Regardless of S.W.'s vivid imagination or characterization of the jump rope given to him by the school as something else, officials saw that it was a jump rope. While he may have been 'twirling it' at officials in what is now described as a 'threatening manner,' he had already been doing that in Wagnon's office, and officials, including Slusser, neither deemed it an exigent circumstance nor tried to physically take the jump rope or restrain S.W."

"Thus, we do not offer an opinion on any other potential issues not before us. Because the district court erred in granting summary judgment, we VACATE and REMAND."

In a concurring opinion, Judge Ho added that "Whether S.W. was denied a reasonable accommodation for his disability under these circumstances has not yet been addressed by the district court in the first instance. Accordingly, I concur in the decision to vacate the judgment and remand this case for further proceedings."

Reversed and remanded.

Outcome: Parent prevailed.

Return to Table of Cases

Spring Ranch Indep. Sch. Dist. v. O.W.
5th Circuit
938 F.3d 695
Judge Brown
9/16/2019 - Texas

In light of the Spring, 2020 coronovirus school closings and possible claims of entitlement to compensatory education, this is a timely case. It cites as authority, two leading compensatory education cases, the 2005 *Reid* case and the 2008 *Draper* case, in the DC and 11th Circuit, respectively.

In this case, the Fifth Circuit explained that "On August 5, 2016, the hearing officer issued a decision in O.W.'s favor on four issues, finding that (1) the School District violated its child find obligation because it did not timely refer O.W. for a special education evaluation; (2) the School District failed to provide O.W. a free appropriate public education (FAPE) for the 2014-2015 academic year because it did not timely fulfill its child find duties, because it violated his IEP by placing him in school for only three hours a day, and because O.W., who was gifted and talented, was failing math; (3) the reduction of hours in May 2015 deprived O.W. of a commensurate school day; and (4) the School District failed to implement O.W.'s IEP because it used restraints, time-outs, and police intervention, and reduced O.W.'s school hours."

"Based on these findings, the hearing officer determined that O.W. was entitled to reimbursement from the School District for $50,250 in tuition and tutoring for O.W.'s enrollment at Fusion for the 2015-2016 academic year, and that O.W. was entitled to a compensatory education award of tuition for Fusion for the 2016-2017 school year."

"On appeal, the School District challenges the district court's conclusions that (1) the School District breached its child find duty with regard to O.W.; (2) the School District failed to fully implement O.W.'s IEP; and (3) two years of private placement tuition was an appropriate remedy for O.W."

With regard to "child find" the Court of Appeals noted that "A finding of a child find violation turns on three inquiries: (1) the date the child find requirement triggered due to notice of a likely disability; (2) the date the child find duty was ultimately satisfied; and (3) the reasonableness of the delay between these two dates."

"We agree with the hearing officer that by October 8, 2014, the School District should have known that general behavior interventions were not working. Accordingly, we conclude the continued use of behavioral interventions was not a proactive step toward compliance with the School District's child find duties and that, therefore, a child find violation occurred."

With regard to FAPE, the Court said that "The parties do not dispute the IEP developed by the School District was adequate in design. However, the hearing officer found, and the district court agreed, the School District failed to implement O.W.'s IEP because it used time-outs, physical restraints, and police involvement as forms of discipline, and because it improperly shortened O.W.'s school day. The School District challenges each of these conclusions."

"In sum, the use of the take-discipline was a significant or substantial departure from O.W.'s IEP. During the time period this departure occurred, O.W. regressed both educationally and behaviorally. Under these circumstances, we conclude the district court did not err in finding an actionable failure to implement O.W.'s IEP as to take discipline."

"O.W.'s disciplinary records show that he was physically restrained eight times and that each instance of restraint was preceded by violent behavior by O.W. and attempts by district staff to utilize at least some of the strategies enumerated in the IEP . . . O.W. does not dispute the uses of restraints were necessary to prevent harm and were thus appropriate under Texas law. Accordingly, the district court erred in concluding these eight instances of physical restraints violated O.W.'s IEP."

"Because the School District took steps to avoid police interaction and O.W.'s behavior posed a substantial risk of serious injury to himself and others, we do not believe the calls to police were inconsistent with O.W.'s IEP. Accordingly, the single instance of police involvement did not rise to the level of an actionable violation."

"[T]he subsequent shortening of O.W.'s school day violated the IEP. This modification, which approximately halved O.W.'s school day, was a substantial and significant deviation from the IEP which indisputably resulted in a loss of academic benefits. Thus, the district court correctly concluded the May 18, 2015, modification rose to the level of an actionable violation."

With regard to the remedy and compensatory education issue, the Court explained that "the right to private school reimbursement, once adjudicated, does not go on indefinitely, but only while the school district is noncompliant (or acknowledges its inability to comply) with its obligation to provide a free appropriate public education."

"[C]ompensatory awards, which may include tuition reimbursement, are designed to provide 'services prospectively to compensate for a past deficient program.' *Draper v. Atlanta Indep. Sch. Sys.*, 518 F.3d 1275, 1280 (11th Cir. 2008). Such awards 'should place children in the position they would have been in but for the violation of the Act.' *Id.* at 1289 (citing *Reid v. District of Columbia*, 401 F.3d 516, 518 (D.C. Cir. 2005))."

"The hearing officer awarded the cost of one year of compensatory education for the 2016-2017 school year at Fusion because '[i]n the 2014-2015 school year, the School District did not timely fulfill its Child Find Obligation and did not fully implement Student's IEP, denying Student a FAPE.' The officer also found the School District should reimburse O.W. for the 2015-2016 school year at Fusion because placement in the School District was inappropriate and placement at Fusion was appropriate. The district court affirmed these decisions."

"To the extent the hearing officer and district court awarded tuition reimbursement for a time period for which there was no corresponding finding of an IDEA violation (the 2015-2016 school year), such an award appears to have been in error. Regardless, because we have determined some of the district court's underlying conclusions were incorrect, we remand the remedy question to the district court for reconsideration in light of this opinion."

"For the reasons above, we AFFIRM in part, REVERSE in part, and REMAND."

Of the three issues raised on appeal, the parents fully prevailed on two and the remedy for the third was remanded back to the District Court for reconsideration.

[**Wrightslaw Note:** The compensatory education, prospective services required, as explained in the *Reid* and *Draper* decisions are critical in future issues related to COVID-19. On our website is a comprehensive article about *Draper* by his two attorneys, Steven Wyner and Marcy Tiffany. ***Draper* article link is here**.]

[**Wrightslaw Note:** Just as this 2019 book was going to press, we learned that on June 12, 2020, the Fifth Circuit, pursuant to a Petition for a Re-Hearing, **withdrew this decision and substituted a new decision**. However, in comparing the September 16, 2019 decision to the new June 12, 2020 decision, the outcome and remedy were unchanged. The parent still prevailed.]

Near the end of the new decision, just above the section titled "IV. Remedies," in the last two sentences of the last paragraph, the Court of Appeals moved one sentence in front of another so that the discussion about the IEP meeting dates listed them in chronological order.

Two new footnotes were added which emphasized that implementation of a 504 Plan was not justification to postpone the initial eligibility process. This failure may have resulted in "a deprivation of educational benefits" which is a factor in the determination of the nature of an award for compensatory education to be considered by the District Court on remand.]

Outcome: Parents prevailed.

Return to Table of Cases

United States v. Florida
11th Circuit
938 F. 3d 1221
Judge Boggs
9/17/2019 - Florida

This is a lengthy, comprehensive decision pitting the United States against the State of Florida in regard to ADA. The initial issue of the case related to the allegation that Florida unnecessarily institutionalized hundreds of children with disabilities in nursing facilities. However, at the District Court level, Florida asserted that the U.S. Attorney General did not have standing to bring the lawsuit. The Eleventh Circuit's opinion is comprehensive, detailed, and includes a Table of Contents as a guide to understanding the interplay between ADA, Section 504 and the Civil Rights Act. This case is not about institutionalization as that aspect was not the issue at this level.

The Eleventh Circuit opened: "In September 2012, after completing a six-month investigation, the Department of Justice issued a Letter of Findings notifying Florida that it was failing to meet its obligations under Title II of the Americans With Disabilities Act of 1990 (ADA) and its implementing regulations, by 'unnecessarily institutionalizing hundreds of children with disabilities in nursing facilities.' The Department of Justice also asserted that Florida's Medicaid policies and practices placed other children who have 'medically complex' conditions, or who are 'medically fragile,' at risk of unnecessary institutionalization."

"The Department of Justice negotiated with Florida to attempt to resolve the violations identified in the Letter of Findings. After concluding that it could not obtain voluntary compliance, the Department of Justice filed suit in the Southern District of Florida in July 2013, seeking declaratory and injunctive relief under Title II of the ADA and 28 C.F.R. § 35.130(d)."

"In December 2013, pursuant to Fed. R. Civ. P. 42(a), the district court consolidated the Department of Justice's suit with a previously-filed class-action complaint from a group of children who similarly alleged that Florida's policies caused, or put them at risk of, unnecessary institutionalization and unlawful segregation on the basis of disability."

". . . Florida filed a Motion for Judgment on the Pleadings, asserting that Title II of the ADA did not authorize the Attorney General to file suit . . . in 2016, the district court . . . dismissed the Department of Justice's case because it concluded that the Attorney General lacked standing to sue under Title II of the ADA. After further litigation, the district court dismissed the children's case. This appeal followed."

Thus the issue on appeal was the power of the Attorney General to file this lawsuit, i.e., whether he had standing.

"It is undisputed that Title II permits a private cause of action for injunctive relief or money damages. [Citing the special education exhaustion of administrative remedies case -] *Fry v. Napoleon Cmty. Schs.*, ___ U.S. ___, 137 S. Ct. 743, 750, 197 L.Ed.2d 46 (2017). We must determine whether Title II's enforcement scheme, 42 U.S.C. § 12133, permits the Attorney General to bring an enforcement action."

"Through a series of cross-references, the enforcement mechanism for Title II of the ADA is ultimately Title VI of the Civil Rights Act of 1964. *See* 42 U.S.C. § 12133; 29 U.S.C. § 794a; 42 U.S.C. § 2000d-1. Section 12133 of Title II states that the 'remedies, procedures, and rights' available to a person alleging discrimination are those available in § 505 of the Rehabilitation Act of 1973, 29 U.S.C. § 794a. Section 505 contains a provision for enforcing § 504 of the Rehabilitation Act, which prohibits discrimination on the basis of disability by programs and activities receiving federal financial assistance. *See* 29 U.S.C. §§ 794(a); 794a." [**Wrightslaw Note:** Section 504 hyperlink here.]

"We are not the first court to pass upon this issue, and a review of other cases that have considered whether Title II permits the Attorney General to file suit demonstrates that the district court's decision is an outlier."

In its conclusion, two of the three judges wrote that "When Congress chose to designate the 'remedies, procedures, and rights' in § 505 of the Rehabilitation Act, which in turn adopted Title VI, as the enforcement provision for Title II of the ADA, Congress created a system of federal enforcement. The express statutory language in Title II adopts federal statutes that use a remedial structure based on investigation of complaints, compliance reviews, negotiation to achieve voluntary compliance, and ultimately enforcement through 'any other means authorized by law' in the event of noncompliance. In the other referenced statutes, the Attorney General may sue. The same is true here."

Dissenting Judge Branch wrote: "Because the United States is not a 'person alleging discrimination' under Title II of the Americans with Disabilities Act (ADA), Title II does not provide the Attorney General of the United States with a cause of action to enforce its priorities against the State of Florida. Accordingly, I respectfully dissent."

The Opinion ended with: "For the foregoing reasons, we REVERSE the district court's judgment and REMAND for proceedings consistent with this opinion."

[**Wrightslaw Note**: Florida subsequently filed an En Banc Petition for Rehearing. On November 20, 2019, pending a ruling as to whether or not to grant a rehearing, the court's mandate has been withheld. The federal government filed their brief in opposition to the Petition on March 20, 2020. As of May 10, 2020 the matter is still pending." For a somewhat similar case, see the July 5, 2019 *Brown v. DCPS* case, linked here.]

Outcome: United States prevailed, Petition for Rehearing is pending.

Return to Table of Cases

Fry v. Napoleon Comm. Sch.
Michigan U.S. District Court
Judge Cox
9/25/2019 – Michigan

This is the U.S. District Court Opinion and Order in the famous *Fry*, "Exhaustion of Administrative Remedies" SCOTUS case based on 20 USC 1415(l).

For background, on December 17, 2012, the parents filed their lawsuit against the school district alleging violations of Section 504 and the ADA. It was dismissed by the District Court and Court of Appeals for the parent's failure to exhaust their administrative remedies as required in the above statute.

On February 22, 2017, the U.S. Supreme Court reversed the Sixth Circuit and remanded the case back to the Court of Appeals which, in 2017 remanded the case back to the District Court (District Court Case No. 12-15507) so that it could "proceed to resolve this case in accordance with the Supreme Court's opinion." Prior to the September 25, 2019 Opinion and Order, the District Court resolved several issues. (*See* 371 F.Supp.3d 387 (2019)). This decision directs that the Frys' claims shall "proceed to a jury trial."

The District Court, in the September 25, 2019 Opinion and Order, explained that the "Plaintiff filed this action against Defendants alleging they violated the Americans with Disabilities Act (ADA) and Section 504 of the Rehabilitation Act (Section 504) by refusing to allow her, a minor student . . . to bring her service dog to school with her. Discovery in this longstanding action has closed and both parties filed summary judgment motions, which were heard by the Court on August 29, 2019. Plaintiff's summary judgment motion asks the Court to rule in her favor as to liability on her intentional discrimination claim, and then schedule a jury trial to determine damages. Defendants filed a summary judgment motion that asks the Court to rule in their favor and dismiss this case. For the reasons set forth below, the Court concludes that neither party is entitled to summary judgment and that Plaintiff's ADA and Section 504 claims shall proceed to a jury trial."

The Court then detailed the legal basis for denying each Motion for Summary Judgment and ordering that the case proceed to a jury.

[**Wrightslaw Note:** As noted in the beginning of this book, our 2017 Year in Review book contains the complete *Fry* decision and the "Transcript of Announcement of the *Fry* Opinion by Justice Kagan."]

[In preparation for the Jury Trial, three weeks later, on October 15, 2019 the District Court Judge issued a forty-four page "Joint Final Pretrial Order" listing the "Plaintiff's Claims," the "Defendant's Claims," the "Stipulated Facts," the "Issues of Fact to be Litigated," the "Issues of Law to be Litigated," the "Evidence Problems Likely to Arise at Trial," each party's "List of Witnesses," "Exhibits" to be submitted by each party and potential objections to each exhibit, "Damages" to be claimed, number of expected days for the "Jury Trial" and "Settlement Discussions" including the amounts demanded and offered, followed by "Trial Briefs and Jury Instructions."]

[**Wrightslaw Note: Below are hyperlinks** to the original Complaint filed in 2012 with the Court, the Supreme Court's February 22, 2017 Opinion, the Pretrial Order, the Settlement Order, and our webpage about the case are below:]

https://www.wrightslaw.com/law/pleadings/fry.complaint.distct.2012.pdf
https://www.wrightslaw.com/law/caselaw/2017/

ussupct.fry.napoleon.15-497.pdf
https://www.wrightslaw.com/law/pleadings/fry.final.pretrial.order.pdf
https://www.wrightslaw.com/law/pleadings/fry.settlement.order.pdf
https://www.wrightslaw.com/law/art/fry.napoleon.504.service.dog.htm

[On November 14, 2019 the case was settled, terms unknown, and a Settlement Order was entered by Judge Cox.]

Outcome: Parent prevailed.

Return to Table of Cases

McMillen v. New Caney Indep. Sch. Dist.
5th Circuit
Judge Costa
10/2/2019 - Texas

This is a *Fry* exhaustion of administrative remedies case in which the Fifth Circuit explained that "we decide for the first time in our circuit whether the IDEA's exhaustion requirement applies when the plaintiff seeks a remedy that the IDEA does not supply . . . [that is] whether the exhaustion requirement applies to this suit seeking damages under the Rehabilitation Act and section 1983 for a student's expulsion from high school."

The facts in this case are that "Chris McMillen was enrolled in New Caney Independent School District from age 4 (pre-kindergarten) until early in his junior year of high school. During those years, the district developed and implemented an individualized education program (IEP) for McMillen, who had been diagnosed with autism spectrum disorder, emotional disturbance, and central-auditory-processing disorder. The program successfully managed his behavioral challenges for several years."

"McMillen's behavior worsened during his sophomore year to the point that he was threatening to harm himself and others daily. The committee overseeing McMillen's IEP met three times that year. By the middle of the year, McMillen was placed in the district's Pass Program, which is for students who have demonstrated either serious emotional disturbance or behavior disorders and have not responded to less intrusive interventions."

The Circuit Court was quite critical of the next steps taken by the school district and by one particular teacher.

"Despite the problems during McMillen's sophomore year, the district returned him to the regular school setting for his junior year. His IEP for his junior year abandoned measures, like participation in the Pass Program, that had proven successful. McMillen's parents complained about the changes, but New Caney refused to amend his IEP. The new plan was woefully inadequate and intentionally indifferent to McMillen's needs."

"McMillen's return to the traditional classroom put him in Margaret Hudman's English class. Hudman tried to 'save' McMillen, in two senses of the word. She encouraged McMillen to take herbal supplements that she thought could cure his autism. She also tried to convert McMillen to Christianity, believing that if he converted his disabilities would be cured."

"About a month into the school year, Hudman gave up and tried to have McMillen expelled. She collected material that McMillen wrote during class and their informal sessions which, taken out of context, made McMillen appear dangerous. Hudman emailed these materials to school administrators, who referred the matter to the school's police department. The police arrested and charged McMillen with the felony of making a terroristic threat. Following McMillen's arrest, the district determined that he should attend an alternative campus."

"McMillen's parents eventually accepted an offer from the county attorney to drop the felony charge in exchange for their agreeing to never return McMillen to the school district. McMillen's parents believed that accepting the deal was the only option and ceased all efforts to return him to New Caney ISD."

"This lawsuit followed . . . which asserts a Rehabilitation Act claim and an equal protection claim under section 1983." The defendants moved to dismiss the case for "failure to exhaust. The district court granted the motion."

On appeal, even though the case was postured as a Section 504 damages case and not an IDEA case, the Fifth Circuit reviewed the *Fry* decision and its language. "The exhaustion requirement is not limited to suits enforcing the IDEA. It applies to suits under any laws that 'seek relief that is also available under' the IDEA."

"Most other circuits addressed this issue pre-*Fry* . . . Interpreting the IDEA to prevent parties from circumventing the scheme that Congress established in section 1415(l) through clever pleading was central to *Fry*. And the Supreme Court's test for exhaustion—whether the lawsuit seeks a free appropriate public education—comports with reading 'relief' to focus on the conduct the plaintiff complains about."

"But both the substance and language of McMillen's complaint reveal that he is challenging the denial of a free appropriate public education. McMillen treats the failure of his 2015-16 IEP as the precipitating event for all that followed his junior year. The IEP was the district 'giving up on Chris'; 'abandoning what had been working'; exhibiting 'negligence, professional negligence and misjudgment, deliberate indifference, and malice towards Chris'; and 'was nothing more than Defendant New Caney ISD and the IEP Team proverbially throwing up their hands and declaring we are tired of dealing with Chris-Twelve years of putting up with him is enough.' The central failing of the IEP is that it removed McMillen from the Pass Program, which 'was designed to work with students who have demonstrated either serious emotional disturbance or behavior disorders, . . . and returned him to the care of professionals who had already proven their inability to manage Chris's Disabilities.'"

In addition to criticizing the teacher who had hoped to cure his autism through conversion to Christianity, the Court also pointed the finger at the school district's ARD Committee. "The IEP thus was the reason McMillen was in the English class where he lasted only about a month before the behavior problems that resulted in the criminal charge. And who was responsible for the problems with the IEP? The 'ARD Committee'—more IDEA lingo meaning the Admission, Review, and Dismissal Committee that Texas schools use to develop and approve IEPs."

The fault was with the ARD Committee, which denied the student FAPE. "We thus conclude that McMillen's lawsuit challenges New Caney ISD's failure to provide him with the free appropriate public education that the IDEA promised him . . . Allowing a plaintiff complaining about the denial of a free appropriate public education to avoid exhaustion 'merely by tacking on a request for money damages' would subvert the procedures Congress designed for prompt resolution of these disputes."

"We therefore hold that the IDEA's exhaustion requirement applies to plaintiffs who seek damages for the denial of a free appropriate public education. Because McMillen did not first seek relief through the IDEA administrative process, this lawsuit was properly dismissed."

Outcome: School prevailed.

Return to the Table of Cases

A.B. v. Clear Creek Indep. Sch. Dist
5th Circuit
10/10/2019 - Texas

This is a Least Restrictive Environment (LRE) mainstreaming case. The school district proposed a change of placement, parents objected and requested a due process hearing, pursuant to stay-put, the child remained in the same placement, parents prevailed before the Hearing Officer and District Court, sued for attorney's fees, and the school appealed the District Court's finding.

The Court discussed the requirements of LRE, relying on *Daniel R.R. v. State Board of Education*, 874 F.2d 1036 (5th Cir.1989), hyperlinked here.

Citing the LRE statute at 20 U.S.C. § 1412(a)(5), the Court explained that "Relevant to this appeal is the IDEA's requirement that states educate children with disabilities in the least restrictive environment: 'To the maximum extent appropriate, children with disabilities . . . [must be] educated with children who are not disabled, and . . . removal of children with disabilities from the regular educational environment [must] occur only when the nature or severity of the disability of a child is such that education in regular classes with the use of supplementary aids and services cannot be achieved satisfactorily.'"

"The district court denied the school district's request that it reverse and vacate the hearing officer's decision, though it reserved judgment as to the attorney's-fees issue. The court found that 'A.B. received positive, nontrivial, academic and nonacademic benefits when placed in a classroom in a general educational setting.' And although A.B. was academically behind his classmates, the court found that 'his progress remained consistent and markedly improved in a general educational setting.' As a result, the court concluded that removing A.B. from the general-education class would be inconsistent with IDEA's least restrictive environment requirement."

"The principal issue in this appeal is whether the school district's proposed placement of A.B. back into the Learning to Learn program would comport with the IDEA's requirement that children be educated in the least restrictive environment. That question is answered in two steps: 'First, we ask whether education in the regular classroom, with the use of supplemental aids and services, can be achieved satisfactorily . . . . If it cannot . . ., we ask, second, whether the school has mainstreamed the child to the maximum extent appropriate. *Daniel R.R. v. State Bd. of Educ.*, 874 F.2d 1036, 1048 (5th Cir. 1989).'"

"Several inquiries inform the determination of whether a school district 'can achieve education in the regular classroom satisfactorily.' *Id.* Preliminarily, we ask 'whether the state has taken steps to accommodate the [child with disabilities] in regular education.' *Id.* This question can be dispositive: 'If the state has made no effort to take such accommodating steps, . . . the state is in violation of the Act.' *Id.* By contrast, 'if the state is providing supplementary aids and services and is modifying its regular education program,' the inquiry becomes "whether the state's efforts are sufficient.' *Id.*"

The District Court "found a lack of evidence that A.B. would 'entirely absorb a teacher's time and create an undue burden, especially with a paraprofessional providing in-class . . . support.' Given these factual findings, the district court was correct to conclude that the school district was able to—and thus was required to—educate A.B. satisfactorily in the general-education environment."

"We ask whether education in the regular classroom, with the use of supplemental aids and services, can be achieved satisfactorily. *Daniel R.R.*, 874 F.2d at 1048. The evidence here is that it could. A.B. does not need to demonstrate that he was receiving a special benefit from the general-education setting in order to merit being placed there; the preference for general education is built into the IDEA. As we said in *Daniel R.R.*, our analysis goes beyond 'whether the student will gain any educational benefit from regular education' because 'educational benefits are not mainstreaming's only virtue.' *Id.* at 1047.

"The record demonstrates that A.B. can be, and has been, educated satisfactorily in the regular classroom. Consequently, his proposed removal to a special-education program would violate IDEA's requirement that students be educated in the 'least restrictive environment.' *See* § 1412(a)(5)(A). The order of the district court is AFFIRMED."

Outcome: Parents prevailed.

Return to the Table of Cases

T.W. v. Dallas Indep. Sch. Dist.
5th Circuit

941 F.3d 224
Judge Haynes
10/25/2019 - Texas

This is a *Fry* exhaustion of administrative remedies case where the IEP child was raped by a classmate and parents sued the district for sex discrimination under Title IX of the Education Amendments Act of 1972, beginning at 20 USC 1681 [**Title IX hyperlink here** - https://www.law.cornell.edu/uscode/text/20/chapter-38]

It states that "No person in the United States shall, on the basis of sex, be excluded from participation in, be denied the benefits of, or be subjected to discrimination under any education program or activity receiving Federal financial assistance."

"Taking the Plaintiff's allegations as true, T.W., a special needs student in Dallas Independent School District, was repeatedly assaulted by a classmate, V.A. T.W. and her case manager, Ms. Gray, notified the school. The school's 'solution' was to move T.W. and V.A. to different parts of the room. V.A. was assigned to a desk in front of the class bathroom. The abuse did not stop. V.A. allegedly raped T.W. in the class bathroom, a foot away from his desk. Doe, T.W.'s mother, withdrew her daughter after finding out about the rape."

"Doe sued Dallas ISD on behalf of T.W., asserting that the school violated T.W.'s rights under Title IX. The district court dismissed Doe's Title IX claim for failure to exhaust her IDEA administrative remedies."

"Though Doe had not sued under the IDEA, the district court concluded that Doe's claim could have been brought as an IDEA claim. It therefore determined that § 1415(l) barred Doe's suit until she exhausted her claim."

"Doe did not appeal that decision and instead attempted to comply with the district court's direction to exhaust her claims. She filed both a Title IX claim and an IDEA claim with a special education hearing officer. The hearing officer dismissed her IDEA claim because the claim was filed well beyond the one-year statute of limitations. The hearing officer also concluded that he lacked jurisdiction to consider the Title IX claim and dismissed that claim."

"Doe then went back to federal court, again asserting only a Title IX claim. In addition to attempting to exhaust her claim, she had the benefit of the recently decided Supreme Court decision, *Fry v. Napoleon Community Schools*. In *Fry*, the Supreme Court held that § 1415(l)'s exhaustion requirement applies only if a plaintiff seeks relief available under the IDEA, which is limited to a student's right to a free appropriate public education (FAPE). Doe claimed that *Fry* clarified that she did not need to administratively exhaust her claim under the IDEA because she did not seek relief related to the denial of a FAPE."

"Dallas ISD moved to dismiss under Federal Rules of Civil Procedure 12(b)(1) and 12(b)(6). The district court again dismissed Doe's claim, concluding that its previous legal reasoning was consistent with *Fry*. Since the hearing officer had dismissed the IDEA claim as time-barred, which did not exhaust the claim, the district court concluded that Doe's Title IX claim, which the court ruled was intertwined with a potential IDEA claim, was also unexhausted under § 1415(l). It dismissed her suit for lack of jurisdiction. Doe now appeals the dismissal of her Title IX claim."

The Fifth Circuit applied *Fry* and explained that "It applies only if a plaintiff 'seeks relief available under the IDEA . . . [which is] limited to a student's right to a FAPE . . . a statutory term of art and is generally centered on a disabled student's access to adequate education by a school. Thus, to determine whether § 1415(l) applies, courts must 'examine whether a plaintiff's complaint . . . seeks relief for the denial of an appropriate education.' *Fry*, 137 S. Ct. at 755. That 'examination should consider substance, not surface. The use (or non-use) of particular labels and terms is not what matters.' *Id.* Instead, it is 'the gravamen of a complaint' that matters. *Id.*'"

"Doe's suit is about sex discrimination; a non-disabled student could have brought Doe's allegation that the school was indifferent to her sexual abuse

. . . there have been numerous Title IX claims brought by students who have made similar allegations of a school's indifference to a student-on-student sexual abuse. Based on the Supreme Court's holding in *Fry*, we hold that Doe did not need to exhaust her administrative remedies under § 1415(l), as the gravamen of her complaint was not about the denial of a FAPE."

"For the foregoing reasons, we REVERSE the district court's grant of Dallas ISD's Rule 12(b)(1) motion to dismiss and REMAND the case for further proceedings consistent with this opinion."

[**Wrightslaw Note**: After the case was remanded back to the District Court, the parents filed an amended complaint which explained in more detail the facts in regard to that incident. After the parents pulled their child out of the school, Dallas charged the mother with truancy and she had to appear in Court at a truancy hearing. The February 7, 2020 Amended Complaint is located on Wrightslaw at: https://www.wrightslaw.com/law/pleadings/tx.complaint.rape.cirkiel.pdf - hyperlinked here.]

In May 2020, several of the Kimball High School staff named in the court opinions and in the Complaint were listed as staff at the High School pursuant to the High School's website.

On March 18, 2020 the District Court entered a Protective Order sealing the records subpoenaed from Child Protective Services.

This case is pending and poised for a jury trial unless settled.

Outcome: Parents and child prevailed.

Return to the Table of Cases

Kimes v. Matayoshi, Hawaii Supt DOE
9th Circuit

10/28/2019 – Hawaii

This was an appeal from a **four-day** Section 504 lawsuit and jury trial related to discipline, restraints, reasonable accommodations and deliberate indifference in which the jury ruled against the parents. Relying on four separate issues, they asked the District Court Judge to set aside the verdict as contrary to law. The Judge refused and parents appealed to the Ninth Circuit.

At that level, the Court explained that "To recover damages on her Rehabilitation Act claim against the Department of Education (DOE), Theresa Kimes was required to show not only that school officials denied R.K. a reasonable accommodation, but also that they did so with deliberate indifference. To prove deliberate indifference, Kimes had to show that DOE (1) knew that its actions would likely result in a violation of R.K.'s right to an equal public education and (2) took those actions anyway. The jury returned a special verdict that found DOE did not act with deliberate indifference. The jury's finding is supported by substantial evidence."

"Second, Kimes alleged that DOE denied R.K. a reasonable accommodation when school officials forcibly restrained her on March 10, 2016. Several witnesses testified that this decision responded to R.K.'s verbal and physical threats to kill herself and occurred after half an hour of attempted de-escalation. The jury could reasonably have concluded that school officials decided to restrain R.K. to protect her, and thus meant to further her right to safe education, not hinder it."

"Third, Kimes alleged that DOE took impermissible disciplinary action against R.K. for behavior stemming from her disability. The Supreme Court has held that, 'where a student poses an immediate threat to the safety of others, officials may temporarily suspend him or her for up to 10 schooldays' without violating the Individuals with Disabilities Education Act. *Honig v. Doe*, 484 U.S. 305, 325 (1988). The jury heard that the disciplinary actions taken against R.K. amounted to no more than two isolated half-day suspensions, both on days when R.K. had acted violently toward others. The jury thus could reasonably have found that DOE believed these suspensions did not violate R.K.'s federally protected rights."

"Fourth, Kimes challenged DOE's decision to prohibit R.K.'s nurse from accompanying her onto campus on March 11, 2016. DOE employees testified that the school had a back-up nurse that day and that officials were in the process of communicating with R.K.'s previous school to request that they send another nurse. This testimony supports a finding that DOE did not know it was likely R.K. would be deprived of her right to a safe education, but rather intended that she receive necessary support from these other nurses."

"Ample evidence supports the jury's determination that DOE was not deliberately indifferent to R.K.'s needs. The district court therefore correctly denied Kimes' motion for judgment notwithstanding the verdict."

[**Wrightslaw Note**: The 25 pages of Jury Instructions and the four-page Jury Verdict are located on Wrightslaw at:
https://www.wrightslaw.com/law/pleadings/hawaii.kimes.504.jury.instructions.pdf - **hyperlinked here**
https://www.wrightslaw.com/law/pleadings/hawaii.kimes.504.jury.verdict.pdf - **hyperlinked here**

Outcome: School prevailed.

Return to the Table of Cases

Pocono Mtn. Sch. Dist. v. T.D.
3rd Circuit
Judge Fisher
10/29/2019 – Pennsylvania

This is a tuition reimbursement case with a dispute regarding whether the tuition reimbursement is due pursuant to IDEA or Section 504. Both parties appealed the District Court's ruling to the Third Circuit. As the case was proceeding through the litigation and appellate process, the school district continued to pay the private school tuition, causing the school's appeal to become moot.

The Third Circuit's ruling is quite brief and does not provide the full history. The July 20, 2018 District Court Opinion by Judge Robert D. Mariani (3:15-CV-764) was very comprehensive and detailed. Portions quoted below explain that "Based on documentary evidence and witness testimony during the administrative hearings, the Hearing Officer found that (1) TD was not eligible for a free and appropriate public education (FAPE) under the Individuals with Disabilities Education Act (IDEA), because he 'does not qualify as a student with a disability under the IDEA'; (2) but TD was disabled (due to his conversion disorder and anxiety disorder) under Section 504 of the Rehabilitation Act of 1973, (Section 504), and that he was denied FAPE under Section 504 as of May 14, 2013, which entitled him to one hour of compensatory education per school day for a period of 26 school days, as well as tuition reimbursement for the 2013-14 and 2014-15 school years; and (3) the District demonstrated deliberate indifference towards TD on the basis of his disability."

"Because the Court finds that TD had an eligible disability under IDEA and was denied FAPE for that disability, TD is separately entitled to tuition reimbursement despite the lack of deliberate difference on the part of the District. While compensatory damages require a finding of deliberate difference under Section 504, there is no such requirement under IDEA."

"More bizarrely, the Objections [filed by school board attorney] include an email from a college professor criticizing the legal reasoning [of the Hearing Officer]. The Court is baffled by the inclusion of a post hoc opinion . . . from a person unrelated to this case. The inclusion of the email is not only irrelevant, but is also, as a general matter, highly inappropriate, as not even expert witnesses involved in the case are permitted to opine on the legal issues of the case. Moreover, the email offers cursory statements with no citations to the record. The Court will therefore disregard any arguments based on the third-party email." (Quotes from the District Court Opinion.)

The Third Circuit explained that "In this case, both

issues raised by the parties—the correctness of the District Court's IDEA eligibility determination and its finding that Pocono did not act with deliberate indifference under § 504—are related to tuition reimbursement and are therefore moot."

"Neither party has a personal stake in the outcome of the claims related to tuition reimbursement, and the relevant issues are moot."

"Because the District Court's IDEA eligibility determination and its deliberate indifference finding bear only on the tuition reimbursement award, we will vacate the District Court's determinations on those issues."

Pocono argued that "the District Court incorrectly awarded twenty-six hours of compensatory education under § 504 without a deliberate indifference finding. Pocono failed to raise this issue in its opening brief, so the issue is waived and the District Court's award of twenty-six hours of compensatory education under § 504 will be affirmed."

"For the foregoing reasons, we will vacate the District Court's IDEA determination and deliberate indifference finding and affirm its award of compensatory education under § 504."

Outcome: Parents and child prevailed.

Return to the Table of Cases

United States Government Accountability Office Report to Congressional Requesters
11/4/2019

GAO issued a report to Congress about "***IDEA Dispute Resolution Activity in Selected States Varied Based on School Districts' Characteristics.***" It is a 28 page report followed by 24 pages of 17 data tables and 3 appendices.

The report is on our website at: https://www.wrightslaw.com/info/gao.idea.dispute.resolution.2019.pdf

"GAO reviewed publicly available data on dispute resolution at the state level and collected data at the school district level from five states—Massachusetts, Michigan, New Jersey, Ohio, and Pennsylvania—selected based on the number of disputes initiated and school district characteristics, among other factors."

They reported that "Parents may face a variety of challenges in using IDEA dispute resolution, and the Department of Education and states provide several kinds of support that, in part, may address some of these challenges. Stakeholders cited challenges such as paying for attorneys and expert witnesses at a due process hearing, parents' reluctance to initiate disputes because they feel disadvantaged by the school district's knowledge and financial resources, and parents' lack of time off from work to attend due process hearings. Education and state agencies provide technical assistance to support parents' understanding of their rights under IDEA and to facilitate their use of dispute resolution options, for example, by providing informational documents and phone help lines to parents."

"While parents may hire an attorney to help with dispute resolution, stakeholders consistently told us the cost of attorneys and expert witnesses was a significant barrier to parents' ability to use the due process complaint option in particular—especially low-income parents. Parents are not required to use an attorney at a due process hearing, but stakeholders told us that prevailing is difficult without legal representation and expert witnesses to testify on the parents' behalf."

"Stakeholders also told us that they are aware of cases in which the school district has called the state's child protective services agency in what they believe was retaliation for parents bringing a dispute against the district, and that parents who are undocumented may fear that raising a dispute might result in unwanted attention from immigration officials."

Return to the Table of Cases

United States v. Nobel Learning Communities
New Jersey District Court

11/13/2019 - New Jersey

This is a New Jersey District Court case that we are including because ADA is having a greater impact in regard to the education of children with disabilities in private schools. This case had several published Opinions in Google Scholar and quotes below are from those Opinions, the Complaint and subsequent Settlement Agreement.

"Defendant Learning Communities (NLC) is the owner and operator of the Chesterbrook Academy (Chesterbrook) in Moorestown, New Jersey. Chesterbrook offers daycare services and an educational foundation program for young children in several states. M.M., born on July 11, 2011 with Down syndrome, enrolled at Chesterbrook Moorestown on January 5, 2012."

"In December 2014, Chesterbrook Moorestown informed M.M.'s parents of its intention to move M.M. into the 'Intermediates' program. At this time, M.M. still required diapers. M.M. was moved into the "Intermediates" program on January 21, 2015. Chesterbrook Moorestown worked with M.M. to try to get her toilet trained, setting a deadline pursuant to their alleged corporate policy for M.M. to be toilet trained by April 1, 2015."

The deadline was not met and the child was expelled.

In regard to another earlier case, referenced in this one "The Court further addressed a January 2011 Settlement Agreement entered between the United States and NLC, which provided that NLC would implement a non-discrimination policy, publicize that policy to its employees, and provide appropriate training, with mandatory reporting to the United States. It also provided NLC would pay $215,000 to the named individuals in the complaint. The Settlement Agreement resolved all of the allegations in the complaint and was to remain in effect for two years."

This case then settled on November 13, 2019 and Nobel Learning, d/b/a Chesterbrook, had to revise, publicize and disseminate their non-discrimination policies and make monetary payments to the parents and the United States in the amount of $18,000 and $30,000 respectively.

Link to the Complaint is here:
https://www.wrightslaw.com/law/pleadings/ada/NJ.ADA.daycare.complaint.pdf
link is here.
Link to the Settlement Agreement is here:
https://www.wrightslaw.com/law/pleadings/ada/NJ.ADA.daycare.settlement.pdf

Outcome: Parents and USDOJ prevailed.

Return to the Table of Cases

Nathan M. v. Harrison Sch. Dist.
10th Circuit
942 F.3d 1034
Judge McHugh
11/14/2019 – Colorado

Like the prior Third Circuit case, this too involved the issue of becoming "moot" because of the passage of time.

The public school proposed moving Nathan from Alpine, a private autism school, paid by the District, into its Otero Elementary School autism program. The parent filed a complaint with the State Department of Education. The State Complaint Officer "found that the District had failed to develop the 2016 IEP in accordance with the IDEA and ordered the District to resume Nathan's placement at Alpine. In response, the District filed a due process complaint . . . [and the parent] filed a counterclaim, alleging the various procedural and substantive violations of the IDEA."

"Ultimately, the ALJ concluded the 'District met its burden of establishing that the 2016 IEP represented an offer of FAPE to Nathan as required under the IDEA and Parent failed to meet her burden of establishing that Nathan was denied FAPE as a result of procedural violations alleged in the development of the IEP."

"Parent appealed the ALJ's decision to the district court . . . [which upheld] ALJ's decision in full."

"Parent timely appealed, [to the Court of Appeals] reasserting the various procedural and substantive IDEA violations she argued before the district court."

"After the appeal had been fully briefed, we requested supplemental briefing from the parties on mootness in light of [the June 12, 2020 Tenth Circuit] *Steven R.F.*, 924 F.3d at 1316, which held moot a similar IEP challenge because the IDEA violations alleged by the parent there were not capable of repetition but evading review . . . Because Nathan has since matriculated from elementary school to middle school, the IEP now recommends he be placed in the Autism program at Mountain Vista Community School instead of the program at Otero. The record does not show whether Parent still opposes this placement."

"Our jurisdiction under Article III extends only to actual, ongoing controversies. The existence of a live case or controversy is a constitutional prerequisite to federal court jurisdiction. If an actual controversy ceases to exist at any stage of litigation, the case has become moot and should be dismissed. Generally, the actual controversy between the parties must exist at all stages of appellate or certiorari review, and not simply at the date the action is initiated."

"The District and Parent do not dispute that Nathan's case is technically moot. Parent initiated this challenge in response to Nathan's 2016 IEP, which 'governed a schoolyear that has passed.' *Steven R.F.*, 924 F.3d at 1313. Any controversy over where Nathan should spend the 2016-17 schoolyear was resolved long ago by operation of the IDEA's 'stay-put' provision, which maintains a child's then-current placement during the pendency of an IEP challenge. 20 U.S.C. § 1415(j) (providing that a 'child shall remain in his then-current educational placement during the pendency of any proceedings conducted pursuant to this section'). Nathan has thus remained at Alpine since 2016, effectively giving Parent the relief she originally sought. Because our present decision about the 2016 IEP can have no effect 'in the real world,' Nathan's case appears to be moot."

"There must exist a continuing controversy between the parties presenting legal questions for resolution, ensuring that our decision on the merits will define the contours of the parties' continuing legal relationship under the IDEA such that future repetitions of the injury could be avoided."

"Parent makes no attempt to show that any alleged procedural violations of the IDEA are capable of repetition. Thus, Parent has seemingly waived any argument that the various procedural violations she alleges are not moot . . . Parent has failed to carry her burden of showing that any of the alleged IDEA violations are likely to recur."

"For these reasons, we VACATE the district court's ruling and REMAND with instructions to dismiss the case as moot."

Outcome: Neither prevailed, case dismissed as moot. However, private school tuition continued to be paid throughout the litigation.

Return to the Table of Cases

Marlboro Bd. Ed. v. H.L.
3rd Circuit
Judge Matey
12/17/2019 – New Jersey

School district failed to exhaust their administrative remedies prior to filing suit in federal court.

The school district was the Plaintiff in the special education due process appeal filed in federal court. In a prior federal court opinion involving the same parties and tuition reimbursement, the Judge remanded the case back to the Administrative Law Judge for further evidence. At that second hearing, the school raised a Motion to Dismiss for parent's failure to participate in a "Resolution Session" and the ALJ refused to grant the Motion pending the submission of evidence.

At that point, prior to a hearing on the merits of the case by the ALJ, the School District appealed to the District Court. "The District Court dismissed the case for lack of jurisdiction, holding that the Board failed to exhaust its administrative remedies. This appeal followed."

Before the Court of Appeals, the school board argued "that one of the exceptions to exhaustion should apply. Again, we disagree. As noted, the ALJ is ready and able to entertain the Board's arguments, so further proceedings would not be futile or inadequate, and may in fact resolve in the Board's favor. The ALJ recognized that the extent of the parents' participation is a question of fact, not law. And the Board does not explain why participation in further agency proceedings would cause any severe or irreparable harm."

"The Board, then, has failed to exhaust its administrative remedies, and cannot rely on any of the exceptions to the exhaustion requirement. The District Court properly dismissed the Board's complaint for lack of jurisdiction. We will therefore affirm."

Outcome: Parents prevailed

Return to the Table of Cases

Bruno v. Northside Indep. Sch. Dist.
5th Circuit
12/17/2019 - Texas

This is a comparable IEP case where a child moved from Florida to Texas. The Fifth Circuit explained that, in Florida, R.B. "attended a full-day, 'mixed' classroom, which is a special-education classroom containing both special-needs and non-disabled students, and received speech and occupational therapy each week. He also received additional services from a private Board Certified Behavior Analyst and occupational therapist."

"Upon enrolling at NISD, the district provided him a temporary service plan designed to furnish R.B. with special-needs services comparable to his Florida IEP as required by IDEA. NISD placed R.B. in a half-day program in a self-contained classroom—a classroom with only special-needs students. His speech-language therapy services and occupational therapy services remained the same as described in his Florida IEP."

After this initial transfer period, NISD completed a Full Individual and Initial Evaluation and developed a new IEP for R.B. In completing the evaluation and developing the new IEP, NISD consulted with R.B.'s parents and teachers, reviewed R.B.'s tests and evaluations from his Florida school district, and relied on evaluations from a speech pathologist, occupational therapist, and licensed specialist in school psychology. NISD determined that R.B. should be provided with less speech and occupational therapy than he had received in Florida and that his classroom should be changed from a self-contained classroom to a mixed classroom."

"On January 11, 2017, Michael and Brittany Bruno, R.B.'s parents, filed a request for a special education due process hearing with the Texas Education Agency. They alleged that NISD committed a substantive violation of the IDEA by denying R.B. a free appropriate public education (FAPE) and committed numerous procedural errors under the IDEA. After a three-day evidentiary hearing, which included testimony from fifteen witnesses and more than 800 pages of exhibits, the special education officer concluded that NISD provided R.B. with a FAPE and did not commit procedural violations of the IDEA. The Brunos appealed the hearing officer's decision to the district court. The district court granted judgment on the administrative record to NISD, and the Brunos appealed to this court."

"We have reviewed the briefs, the applicable law, and relevant parts of the record, and we have heard oral argument. The district court committed no reversible error. The judgment is affirmed, essentially on the basis carefully explained by the district court in its 41-page December 12, 2018 Order."

Outcome: School prevailed.

Return to the Table of Cases

Wofford v. North Little Rock Sch. Dist.

8th Circuit
12/20/2019 – Arkansas

The Eighth Circuit Decision is very short, consisting of one paragraph, upholding the denial of attorneys' fees even though the parent's attorney prevailed at the due process hearing.

To understand the facts, we reviewed the District Court ruling. On March 7, 2019 in "Case No. 4:16-CV-00770" District Court Judge Miller explained that on August 1, 2016 the parents prevailed in a special education due process hearing. "The HO ordered the District to develop an IEP for school year 2016-17 . . . [but Wofford] moved out of the District before the HO's order could be implemented" thus not entitled to attorneys' fees. Case dismissed at the District Court level.

The Fifth Circuit upheld the dismissal noting that "Specifically, as the relief ordered by the hearing officer required Wofford's action, which he did not take before moving J.W. out of the district and precluding implementation of the relief, Wofford cannot be considered a prevailing party."

Outcome: School prevailed.

Return to the Table of Cases

***Ramsay v. National Board of Medical Examiner*s**
Pennsylvania District Court
PA
District Court Judge Joyner
12/30/2019 - PA

Like the earlier November 13, 2019 District Court day care, ADA case, we are including this Pennsylvania District Court case because ADA is having a greater impact in higher education and in the examination and licensing of professionals.

Jessica Ramsay is a medical student in the Homer Stryker M.D. School of Medicine of Western Michigan University (WMed). Defendant National Board of Medical Examiners (NBME) is a non-profit corporation with its principal place of business in Pennsylvania.

"NBME develops a series of standardized timed examinations that are known collectively as the United States Medical Licensing Examination (USMLE) and which are largely in written format. NBME administers these examinations through a third-party-vendor throughout the United States and these examinations are relied upon by states throughout the country in making decisions regarding medical licensure. In order to receive the degree of Doctor of Medicine (i.e. M.D.), to apply and/or be considered for medical residency training programs, and to become licensed as a physician, medical students must first take and pass all of the USMLE 'Step' examinations."

"In March 2009, during her sophomore year at Ohio State University, Plaintiff was diagnosed with Attention Deficit Hyperactivity Disorder, Migraine Headaches and probable dyslexia."

She received numerous accommodations. "Among the examinations for which Plaintiff has received these accommodations during her medical school career are a number of subject matter examinations developed by NBME."

"While a third-year medical student and in anticipation of having to sit for the Step 1 USMLE, Plaintiff applied to NBME for test accommodations, seeking many of the same accommodations that she had been receiving from Western Michigan University Medical School and Ohio State University."

NBME denied her request. "Plaintiff took the Step 1 examination in July 2017 without accommodations with the hope that she could pass and enter into her fourth year of medical school. In so doing, Plaintiff was unable to read all of the questions in each testing "block" which required her to guess at the answers to those remaining questions that she did not have time to read. Plaintiff failed the examination by one point."

She re-applied several times submitting additional documentation each time. Her requests were denied. The Court heard from expert witnesses in regard to dyslexia and ADHD and wrote "To show a violation of the ADA based on a failure to accommodate, a Plaintiff must prove: (1) that she is disabled; (2) that her requests for accommodation are reasonable; and (3) that those requests have been denied. In this case, there is no dispute as to the reasonableness of Plaintiff's requested accommodations nor is there any question but that her request has been denied. Consequently, the threshold issues before us for adjudication are whether or not the Plaintiff truly is disabled and, of course, whether the pre-requisites for issuance of a preliminary injunction have been satisfied."

"It further appears that NBME either discounted or disregarded entirely the admonition to focus on 'how a major life activity is substantially limited, and not on what outcomes an individual can achieve' and apparently ignored the example that someone with a learning disability may achieve a high level of academic success, but may nevertheless be substantially limited in the major life activity of learning because of the additional time or effort he or she must spend to read, write, or learn compared to most people in the general population."

The Judge granted the injunction against NBME and ordered them to provide her with the accommodations.

Link to the federal court Complaint is here - https://www.wrightslaw.com/law/pleadings/ada/PA.ADA.complaint.med.board.pdf

Link to the federal court decision by Judge Joyner is here - https://www.wrightslaw.com/law/caselaw/2019/pa.order.ramsay.504.ada.pdf

NBME has appealed to the Third Circuit. That decision will be in our 2020 "Year in Review" book.

Outcome: Student prevailed.

Return to the Table of Cases

Return to the Beginning of Table of Cases

END
of
Court of Appeals
Special Education / IDEA / 504 cases

Index

Index

LEGAL REFERENCE/EDUCATION

Wrightslaw Special Education Legal Developments and Cases 2019 is designed to make it easier for you to stay up-to-date on new cases and developments in special education law.

Learn about current and emerging issues in special education law, including:

All decisions in IDEA and Section 504 ADA cases by U.S. Courts of Appeals in 2019

How Courts of Appeals are interpreting the two 2017 decisions by the U.S. Supreme Court

Cases about discrimination in a daycare center, private schools, higher education, discrimination by licensing boards in national testing, damages, higher standards for IEPs and "least restrictive environment"

Tutorial about how to find relevant state and federal cases using your unique search terms

About the Authors

Pete Wright, Esq. and Pamela Wright, MA, MSW, are co-founders of Wrightslaw.com and co-sponsors of the Institute of Special Education Advocacy at the William & Mary Law School.

The Wright's co-authored several best-selling books: ***Wrightslaw: Special Education Law, From Emotions to Advocacy, All About IEPs, All About Tests and Assessments and Wrightslaw: Special Education Legal Developments and Cases for 2015, 2016, 2017, and 2018.***

$19.95
ISBN 978-1-892320-49-0
51995>
9 781892 320490

HARBOR HOUSE LAW PRESS, INC.
Hartfield, Virginia
www.harborhouselaw.com

Made in United States
North Haven, CT
12 November 2026

22198991R00070